THE APOCALYPSE OF HISTORY

THE APOCALYPSE
OF HISTORY

Problems of
Providence and Human Destiny

by

E. LAMPERT
D. Phil. Oxon.

IN MY END IS MY BEGINNING
(Inscription on the Chair of State
of Mary Queen of Scots)

FABER AND FABER LTD
24 Russell Square
London

First published in mcmxlviii
by Faber and Faber Limited
24 Russell Square London W.C.1
Printed in Great Britain by
Latimer Trend & Co Ltd Plymouth
All rights reserved

I wish to express my gratitude to Charles H. Vereker for his many helpful comments, criticisms and suggestions both as to the matter and manner of this book. My thanks are also due to Patrick McLaughlin who read the typescript.

E. L.

CONTENTS

I. THE END

II. THE BEGINNING AND THE END

Contents

III. SYMBOLS OF SURVIVAL

Part 1

THE END

Chapter I

APOCALYPSE (Introductory)

There is a book in the New Testament which has always evoked distrust and has been kept dark by those who felt uneasy about it—a book behind whose every word there is a deed, and fire, and terror, and joy. This book is the Apocalypse. It does not speak or inform us only about unusual happenings in the future, but denotes an action, a breaking of the *End* into the midst of History. But men prefer not to be reminded of the End, though they may unwillingly testify to it. Admittedly, there exists a voluminous literature of the commentaries on the Apocalypse, but this does not contribute much to the understanding of the unusual document. It presents what is, more often than not, a superficial exegesis which explains the Apocalypse away in terms of 'influences' and 'borrowings' or amounts to a series of arbitrary interpretations of the apocalyptic symbolism: in both cases it is characterized by an astounding, bewildered and meticulously erudite lack of insight. Only a few have lent an ear to the whispers and the roars of the Apocalypse —to its shattered worlds and its terrible predictions; and many who have done so were driven to exclaim, Blessed are the ears that have heard nothing of the apocalypse of God and man!

Apocalypse means revelation: it reveals the mysterious pathways of evil, of the advent of Anti-christ, of the destruction and cataclysmic transformation of the world; it testifies the greatness and the awfulness of man; it speaks of a final judgment and the disclosure of all things in God and of God in all things. There is nothing in it that may put man's conscience at ease or provide him with 'spiritual comfort', though without its message the heart of mankind would probably fail it. Its philosophy is the philosophy of History. The course of History has always run over volcanic ground and it has been periodically engulfed in lava. History is always threatened and redeemed by its own End. This eschatological fact, the awareness, that is, of the

The End

coming end within History, is particularly evident in catastrophic eras, in wars and revolutions, and in the crises of cultures and civilizations. Some have detected an almost exact analogy between the prevailing mood in such eras and the experience in the life of human individuals who fall under the sway of intense eschatological moods in moments of great ordeals, or suffering, or approaching death. Similarly, people experience the end of the world when an historical age, which they cherish or with which they are intimately associated, is drawing to its close, when a stable order is collapsing and their social status is imperilled. Indeed, 'men are apt to abuse predictions concerning the coming Anti-christ, especially when something does not suit those who are implicated in the evils of the closing age. "We live in an apocalyptic age"—one hears from people who do not believe in any apocalypse whatsoever.' (Berdyaev) One thing is certain: we are contemporaries of extraordinary and momentous historical commotions, and even if, as survivors, we may smile complacently when we realize the narrowness of our escape, we are yet thrown into a whirlpool of events and happenings which drive us to ask ourselves about their meaning and ultimate relations with one another. It is not even a question of a situation *in* which we find ourselves: we ourselves, as it were, are that situation. When the earth is crumbling under men's feet, as it has done so persistently in the present age—however much he may try to drown his awareness in the flux of Time or rely confidently on the permanence of 'civilization', 'progress' and 'evolution'—the bubbles of his complacency are already punctured and he is brought face to face with the ultimate issues of his historic hour; he is pressed to ask—perhaps in desperation—about the meaning of his predicament. There is doubtless much in this predicament that is devoid of any obvious meaning: may it not be that the crux of the situation lies in that it is, in fact, without a meaning, or that it is Meaning's ultimate destruction? May it not be that we are blindly involved in an historical manœuvre the significance of which is essentially beyond our experience? Nevertheless, the deeper the stirring and the greater the confusion, the more intense the longing of all those involved to have at least a glimpse of the final outcome.

It is the business of all who live consciously to admit and to explain the fact of such a longing. A crowd of problems, therefore, presses in upon us, problems that are issues of life and death

rather than of accepting this or that religious, ethical or metaphysical proposition: on the way these problems are tackled or
resolved depends our very existence. What is the purpose of
man's broken and afflicted historic pathways? Do they spring
from some deep and ineffable source, do they move towards
some event of absolute and decisive significance, or are they a
fortuitous and pointless game with no beginning or centre or
end? Does the apparently failing course of History and Time,
like the phantom of the infinite, endless succession of ages, go
on and on into the waste of nothingness, or is it, on the contrary,
in each and every phase capable of transcending itself and revealing a destiny? Can we, at a time when human life—indeed
the human fabric itself—hangs by a hair, go on speaking hon-
estly, and not merely as parsons and people who use phrases
without wisdom sometimes talk, of some ultimate provision, in
fact, of God's providence—that silent mystery rising like a
hieroglyph of fate and the riddle of the sphinx in which man is
to divine his destiny? To face these and such like questions
consciously is to live and think in open recognition of the
Apocalypse as perhaps the most intensely relevant document in
the annals of divine and human ways.

Chapter II

MAN IN TIME

Man's existence is existence in Time; and Time is that material into which the apocalyptic sparks must and do fall in order to reveal its meaning. Such is the original conviction and basic concern of the present essay; and it is born of a realization that to live historically and to apprehend History is to be aware of its *End*, to know 'the ends of Time'.

There is a department in Christian theology which bears the title 'Eschatology' and deals with the 'last things'. It claims to speak of the ultimate future of man and of certain facts which are to occur 'in the last times' or last in Time (a seemingly contradictory notion!) from which we are, however, still happily far off and remote. Such an eschatology represents no more than—in the apt phrase of Karl Barth—innocent little chapters at the very end of Christian dogmatics far from any immediate concern for human life and human consciousness. Few realize that, in point of fact, eschatology is not the teaching about the last things after everything else but rather the teaching about the relation of all things to the 'last things' or, as it were, about the lastness of all things. It traces human existence to its last confines, to its 'crisis', and hence stands as much at the beginning as at the end, as well as at the centre, of our whole Christian faith. It requires an attitude of mind sustained by a constant awareness of an End intensely present and powerful in the here and now of man's historical existence and imbues this existence with meaning. When and where we are ready or bold enough to think and live consistently *to the end* we reach out every time to that final boundary where our lives are transcended into life eternal, to the Lord of Time, and in so doing we are living eschatologically: our History becomes not merely a series of happenings but the disclosure and consummation of divine and human destiny, that is, apocalypse.

Man in Time

These preliminary remarks require further elucidation, but they will suffice, perhaps, to introduce us to a constructive discussion of the first problem which arises in any attempt to interpret the nature of History. How can we find the terms in which the relation of the 'End', of the 'world to come' to Time, to 'this world', can be adequately expressed? How do we apprehend the great and spellbound mystery of Time?

The conception of Time has undergone many changes. When men believed themselves to live in the conditions of an immutable cosmic hierarchy or a stable and untroubled order of things their experience of Time differed considerably from that of men who exist under the impact of world-wide conflagrations, when life proceeds by sudden leaps and bounds rather than by slow and gradual evolution. The mental attitude of past generations tended to conceive Time as a self-contained entity. It was pictured as an infinitely long, a beginningless and endless line on which the *Now* is moving forward from point to point. It resembled a track on which the wain of world-space takes its course, or a road on which a tired wanderer covers his successive distances—one mile after another. The track or road remains a fixed, immutable entity firmly riveted in its entirety and its particularity. Our lives and our experiences, the beating of our hearts and the work of our hands are measured by that immovable order within which Time is bounded. Time is thus the self-sufficient form of a cosmic order or system incapable of pointing beyond itself and for this very reason without meaning within itself. Time does not press any questions on us, nor can we press any questions on Time.

If then, on this premise, we ask ourselves whither the course leads, or what the future has in store for my own and the world's destiny, there are two possible answers. We can either attempt to break out of Time and save ourselves in a supra-temporal sphere, while the stream of temporal happenings continues to flow into infinity; or else we may try to remain within the line of successive temporal moments, transferring the centre of gravity of our existence on to a temporal future which will be the straight and direct continuation of this successive series.

As a matter of fact, both attitudes roughly summarize a variety of conceptions familiar to the student of philosophy, and they have deeply affected the thought of men and even of types of civilization.

The End

(a) Greek Conceptions

It has been rightly said that the ancient Greeks neither knew the use nor felt the absence of the Time-element. Indeed, it is astounding to what an extent Hellenic thought was unable to represent Time otherwise than spatially and by extension, that is to say, through the symbols of physical motion; while motion itself had been conceived as *alloiosis*, change in the position of bodies rather than a 'process', a 'going on', which imples direction or orientation. Time, *chronos*, represents thus a series of 'countable', reversible and divisible points, wholly stationary in themselves but perceived in an unremitting movement of succession—a kind of juxtaposition of quantitative states. This is expressed in the famous argument of Zeno the Eleatic. At any given instant, Zeno argued, a flying arrow is not in motion: it is at rest, occupying the space equal to itself in which it is situated, so that if Time is nothing but a sum of instants the arrow is never in motion at all. A similar interpretation is given by Aristotle.[1] In Plato's view Time coincides with the spatial motion of the stars. The sun is *metron energes* which supplies the *arithmos* whereby Time is to be known.

The spatial conception of Time as in *chronos* prompted yet another symbol expressive of the Classical outlook, namely *cyclos*. Time is the wheeling of perpetual recurrence, a cyclic movement which yet entails no real change, for, like the planetary course, it returns incessantly on itself. Time, 'the moving image of eternity', is the effluence of planets, 'the instruments by which Time is caused'; and though, unlike the heavenly calm and harmony, the circlings of human life are 'confused and wandering', we are drowned in the perpetual cycle of invariable and ultimately meaningless facts, the same everywhere and always, of birth, and hunger, and decay, and death. There is, admittedly, a partial truth in this experience of Time, as everyone who has lived through intense suffering will know: Time seems to revolve, to circle round one centre of pain and to communicate itself as such to all life. And yet even while we experience this inflexible, paralysing immobility of life we find hidden somewhere something that tells us that nothing in the whole world is meaningless, and suffering least of all. This awareness is the point where suffering reaches out beyond the

[1] See, e.g., *Nic. Ethics*, 1174 a 20; or *Physics*, Δ 2196.

16

waste of circling moods. Did the Greeks ever realize that precisely the facts of birth, of hunger and death were to become decisive conditions for the redemption of mankind: the birth of God and Man; hunger assuaged by God's flesh and blood; and death made the promise of risen life? Maybe they did so in their Mysteries, but hardly in their philosophy.

Time on this view must needs be devoid of meaning: through indefinite repetition of cyclic changes it always reverts to the same point, incapable of bursting its fixed confines or of transcending itself. Time such as this is indeed the symbol and embodiment of death; and Eternity, therefore, was necessarily seen and experienced as the absence of Time. No wonder that Aristotle was compelled to exclude from God's eternal intellectual being any contact with the world of Time and becoming and devise the barren idea of a divine knowledge with no other object but itself. His great conception of *entelecheia* is essentially non-historic and timeless—perhaps the only timeless evolution-idea in the history of philosophy. Plato who, unlike Aristotle, possessed a deep awareness of, and humility before, the secret of living things, was still able to perceive an 'up' or 'down', a 'near' or 'far' between the heavenly and earthly things, while Aristotle conceptualized the Classical image of Time and construed a system in which man, fixed in and looking out from his sublunar world, is a necessary part of a total rational universe, of a closed unbroken circle of being which has its completion in divine, absolute perfection. Hence the fundamental difference in tone between Plato, who lent a shuddering ear to Mysteries and knew the meaning of Initiation, and Aristotle who forsook the Mysterious.[1]

True, Greek thought did attempt in certain ways to relate the temporal world to the eternal order, notably in the later Platonic idea of a *demiourgos* and in the more abstract Aristotelian notion of *ousia* and *entelecheia*; but its very conception of Time allowed of no other way to overcome the torments and tragedy of the Time-process than by assuming two disparate and irre-

[1] Plato's muse, however, had two aspects, expressed in the two Socrates who inspired him: a legendary Socrates, informed by the spirit of Orpheus, whose 'Lake of Memory' gave rise to the mystical conception of *anamnesis*; and the other Socrates, commemorated by Xenophon in the *Memorabilia*, a 'midwife', never herself giving birth, the man who, when his days and hours were numbered, refused to be initiated into Mysteries and never stopped talking—probably the real Socrates.

concilable realms, the temporal and the eternal, and by escaping the fiery wheel of temporality: in other words, by seeking for what is meaningful outside and above History, in the eternal repose of divine unchangeableness.[1] We cannot, the Stoics taught, look for any 'new world', positively related to History, in which the conditions of life would be radically different from what they are now. Hence the melting mood of disillusionment and despair which overcasts the luminous face of the Greek Olympus, a mood which was so evidenced by the disappointed decadents of the post-Periclean age. Hence, furthermore, the striking absence of historic sense in ancient Greece: for mere history-writing such as that of Thucydides, or Xenophon, or Polybius, however truthful and masterly in making alive the factual happenings (Thucydides's *History of the Twenty-Seven Years' War* is, admittedly, a great work of art), does not contribute much to the *understanding* of History and is quite ineffectual in face of historic perspectives and motivations.[2]

(b) Idealist Conceptions

Since we are not concerned here with a detailed discussion of the development of the conception of Time throughout the ages, but merely with illustrating certain typical variations on the first answer to the opening question of this section, we may be permitted now to leap into a wholly new intellectual world which is yet, in the last analysis, characterized by the same experience of Time as that of Hellenism, viz., modern Idealist philosophy.

Kant's primary concern was to show the *a priori* character of Time, the *qualitas originaria sensualitatis humanae*. 'Time is nothing but the form of inner sense . . .', 'the purely subjective condition

---

[1] Cf. the similar but even more radically consistent attitude of Indian thought in the *Upanishads*, one of the greatest documents in the annals of the human spirit, and in the systems of the Vedanta and Yogi. *Isvara*, the Lord God, reigns in the utterly unmoved remoteness of his eternal bliss; deep below, in *samsara*, roars the stream of senseless worldly and human existence in perpetually recurring cycles of coming and ceasing. Hence the complete absence of 'events', of dates (and even of clocks!) in the history of Indian civilization. History just happened here, like a dream, and it was more or less artificially reconstructed by Europeans (see Spengler's characterization of Indian culture in *The Decline of the West*, vol. 1).

[2] Aristotle dismisses History as *spoudaioteron* (trivial) because, as he puts it, it presents particulars and not generalities! (Cf. *Poetics* 1452 b.)

Man in Time

of our human perception (Anschauung)', 'pure form of all sensible knowledge' (*Critique of Pure Reason,* Section on Time in 'Transcendental Aesthetic'). Time is, like Space, 'only in the senses'. No absolute reality can be ascribed to it. It is real only as an instrument for the shaping of things in us and by us. As such it fulfils an important task, since it is through Time (and Space) that we make 'synthetic judgments *a priori*', i.e., through it we know. But it is real only as a form of our sensual perceptions. Man does not, ultimately speaking, live in Time. The sphere of Time remains within the limits of the world of mere phenomena, which is as it were the outer region of human existence, the sphere to which belongs the periphery of man—his 'empirical character'. But man possesses also and above all an 'intelligible character' of which the empirical one is 'but the sensual pattern' and which does not know any valid 'before' or 'after'. Every action, irrespective of temporal conditions, to which the phenomena belong, is the immediate effect of the intelligible character of Mind acting freely and out of relation with the temporal order of things (ibid. and throughout the 'Transcendental Dialectic'). Time is 'not a determination of things in themselves but only of our sensibility.' (ibid.) In all Kant's utterances concerning Time the mysterious symbols 'past' and 'future' are hardly mentioned; his concern is rather to show the autonomy and freedom of man in regard to and over against any 'timeliness'. To act freely is to act in one's 'pure' will outside and beyond Time.

We shall not insist here on the epistemological difficulties which are entailed in such a dualism of the temporal and the eternal.[1] Our question is rather whether this view reaches the target at which it seems to aim, namely at the heart of human existence. As a matter of fact such a duplication of man's being lies at the basis of a most important and widespread tendency in the doctrine of man, which extends, with all the differences of emphasis and conclusion, from Plato through medieval scholasticism to the philosophical systems of the Enlightenment: only a few did know of the mysteries attending the temporal destiny of man. We are, in fact, confronted with an outlook

---

[1] After all the real problem of epistemology is precisely the relation of the eternal forms of Mind, which are supposed to vindicate the validity of knowledge, to the knowing man who exists in the concrete realm of Time— a relation which Kant does not really explain.

The End

which must inevitably result in a depreciation of Time and all temporal reality, giving them the character of something worthless, inessential and indifferent; they shrink into meaninglessness in face of the abstractions and generalities of the Idealist subject. We can see this among other things, in Kant's tentative attempt at a philosophy of History. He was prepared to assign a quasi-scientific character to the historical investigation of empirical data, while History itself remained for him a hotch-potch of 'sensual' and 'ideal' tendencies where the real and the true pertains only to the eternal laws of Mind: these lie at the basis of genuine human society but find only their 'illustration', not their 'demonstration', in the confused processes of History. Man, according to the true nature of his autonomous moral self, stands not in History, nor in Time, but in the Absolute and the Eternal, whence he looks on the temporal course of events and from whence he is to build up the Kingdom of God ('*Religion innerhalb der Grenzen der blossen Vernunft*!')[1] He can afford to be cheerful when his thoughts lead him from things as they are to things as they ought to be, from facts to norms.

A powerful attempt to find a true synthesis of Eternity and Time was undertaken by Hegel in his *Logic* and his *Philosophy of History*. His attempt has, undoubtedly, shattered once for all the dualistic system of ancient Classicism. We see how the Absolute, Spirit, Mind enter the great movements of Time. 'Sie (Time) ist das Sein, das, indem es ist, nicht ist, und indem es nicht ist, ist; das angeschaute Werden.' All that is real is subject to the all-producing Chronos who continuously devours his own productions. Since it bears within itself the contradictions of finality it must necessarily succumb to the forces of Time. Yet only the 'real' is under the dominance of becoming in Time, not however the 'concept' (*Begriff*) which is the form of the self-thinking Mind and the essence of Spirit. Spirit, Idea are eternal and Time has no power over them.[2] Hegel had, of course, a greater and more intense awareness and appreciation

---

[1] Cf. Fichte's exclamation in *Anweisungen zum seligen Leben*: 'I am eternal and defy your (world, Time, History) might!'

[2] Cf. B. Croce, *Hegel*, p. 76: 'L'esprit est developpement, est histoire et par cela même être et non-être à la fois, devenir, mais l'esprit *sub specie aeternitatis*, que considère la philosophie, est histoire idéal, éternelle en dehors du temps; il est la série des formes éternelles de ce naître et mourir qui, comme le disait Hegel, ne naît et ne meurt pas' (quoted by F. H. Brabant, *Time and Eternity in Christian Thought*).

of Time than Kant: for the eternal is manifested in becoming and hence can only be perceived or visualized in Time. But, fundamentally, the position is not very far removed from that of Kant. The ground of human existence is wholly relegated to the *a priori*-regions, to the eternal in the face of which Time loses its distinctive character and is nothing but an instrument of the Idea which develops itself through the three dialectical stages of thesis, antithesis, and synthesis.

For some Hegelians such as Bradley (if indeed he can be called a Hegelian) the idea of a real thing in Time is altogether devoid of meaning;[1] they look on Time as unreality riddled with the contradictions of all that changes and quite alien to truth which is always and wholly itself. History, therefore, belongs to the world of appearance. Bosanquet in his *The Meeting of Extremes in Contemporary Philosophy* attacked the Neo-Hegelians because he believed them to surrender the eternity of the Absolute and dissolve it in Time. In point of fact, however, despite the oft quoted Neo-Hegelian dictum 'philosophy is History' which repudiates the 'block universe' and excludes any doctrine of Time and change as only appearances, the new Hegelianism itself admits of no reality except that of transcendent Mind, though this be not the mind of substance (as in classic Idealism) but that of activity. Gentile, for instance, explicitly opposes the transcendental self, the true subject of reality, to all 'empirical selfs' of temporal experience which are not really subsistent subjects but are resolved into a more or less shadowy reflection or projection of the transcendental ego.[2]

There are some modern thinkers who were able to challenge the claims of the Idealists because they thought and lived fully in the predicament of their historic moment and could not avoid mighty impressions from its transcendent forces. Dilthey was one of the most important philosophers led to a conscious opposition to Idealism in its approach to the problem of man's existence in Time, and he has shown the vast implications of

---

[1] Cf. the dangerous half-truths in Bradley's *Essays on Truth and Reality*, p. 468: 'Our world and every other possible world are from one side worthless equally. As regions of mere fact and event they all alike have no value. It counts for nothing where or when such existence is taken to have its place, the difference of past and future, of dreaming and waking, of 'on earth' or elsewhere, are one and all immaterial. Our life has value only because and in so far as it realizes in fact that which transcends time and existence.'

[2] See *Theory of Mind as Pure Act*, p. 18 ff.

The End

History as a real key to the understanding of man.[1] He wanted to see man as he is on this side of the abstractions of the human brain which depotentiate life, beyond the simplifications of speculative thought which destroy the complex unity of man's being embodied as it is in the depth of 'timeliness' and fulfilling in Time its unfathomable destiny. 'Our aim is to describe life.' We cannot understand human existence by disengaging it from temporal and spatial situations, and by elevating it to the frigid and lonely heights of bloodless Ideas, in the belief that this will disclose man's eternal, real being; it is, on the contrary, only made possible by acknowledging his inherent participation in the historical, social and cultural pathways of his age. Time is not an 'Idea': no effort of ours can detach us from the stream of temporality. And even while we imagine ourselves to be on the bank of the stream or as observing it from above or outside, we still remain under the power of its perpetual flux. We are, therefore, quite unable to grasp the true nature of temporal existence and every attempt to do so must needs be destructive of Time itself: it arrests the flux and immobilizes life.

With Kant Time had been rendered almost entirely worthless, while value had been ascribed solely to the 'intelligible' self and the timeless *a priori*-laws of Mind. With Hegel Time had been subsumed in the fulness of the Absolute. Now, with Dilthey, a complete re-orientation is setting in: Eternity seems to disappear entirely from the horizon of human existence and all things are swallowed up in the transient flux of Time. Vita motus perpetuus. This is astounding enough, for we have arrived at the opposite pole. History works with mere psychological motivation: we can no longer transcend the realm of Time in any sense or perceive its meaning, and we are urged to commit ourselves to its unlimited and sovereign rights. We have arrived at nihilism which kills what it feeds on and recoils upon its authors with annihilating force, of which Dilthey himself seems to have been fully aware.[2] Again and again Dilthey compels us to doubt radically all attempts at interpreting the experience of mankind. 'For all generations of thinking and creating men seek to read in the mysterious, unfathomable face of life with its smiling lips and melancholy eyes, yet even this can-

[1] His philosophy is now accessible to English readers through the brilliant introduction by Prof. H. A. Hodges, *Wilhelm Dilthey*.
[2] Cf. Hodges, op cit., p. 33.

not ever be attained' (Works, VI, 287). The realization of issue-less tragedy is the final knowledge about human existence (ibid. V, 109). Nietzsche, who had many things in common with Dilthey, though their temperaments differed, saw life and the movements of life in similar terms: he saw men in the midst of life's floods and whirlpools unprotected by any of the safety devices with which Idealism sought to ensure them against this deadly avalanche. To escape complete nihilism he had, therefore, to take refuge in the dubiously comforting thought of eternal recurrence—that conception of Time returning upon itself and repeating its processes in cycles which issued from the Hellenic experience of life—in which nobody really believed but to which Nietzsche himself clutched fast, lest the feeling of his mission should slip out of him.

And yet, significantly enough, even Dilthey construed his vision into an abstract metaphysical pattern—as soon as he attempted to ask the ultimate question. He spoke of some 'unfathomable connections' (*unergruendliche Zusammenhaenge*) of 'experienced life', of a vision *sub specie aeterni*. He evoked the transcendental 'Spirit, in its uniqueness and its unity in the Divine' (ibid. V, 24). Indeed, here and there we seem to find fundamentally the same attitude as in Hegel. Human existence, according to Dilthey, is grounded in 'metaphysical consciousness', eternal and unchangeable, which, as a matter of fact, inevitably calls for comparison with the Idealist *Bewusstsein ueberhaupt* or the *Wesenheiten* of Husserlian phenomenology. In his true nature man is one 'with the infinite connections of all things, with universal Spirit and the soul of Nature' (ibid. VI, 295). Thus Dilthey too had been unable to reach out to an understanding of the nature of Time except within the framework of the transcendental superstructures of the Idealists through whose eyes human existence is deprived of its validity. And, contrary to his original concern to take Time seriously, all things temporal once more acquire the character of 'mere' symbols, of shells and reflected images.[1] It would seem, indeed, that

---

[1] It is interesting that even Bergson, whose philosophy stands in many respects at the opposite extreme to Idealism, and who had an amazing insight into the nature of Time, reverts nonetheless to a certain abstract monism by which Time is, so to say, disembodied—pure *durée*, with no things that change or things that move but mere change or movement, 'with nothing to support it from below and nothing to guide it from above' (see F. H. Brabant, op. cit., p. 119). This, no doubt, explains Bergson's

The End

German philosophy as a whole is constantly and fatally threatened by a kind of monophysitism (in the widest sense of this Christological term), by a temptation to remove the 'kingdom of heaven' into a transcendental sphere. This sphere remains, in the last resort, unrelated to the natural and historical fabric of human life and activity, unless it be by absorption or subsumption, though it may stimulate man to strive towards, and even to assert himself titanically in, a constant effort in the direction of that kingdom or set him tyrannically towards the future purpose of organizing everybody and everything. . . . From out of the lofty self-assurance of the transcendental self the Idealist subject then proceeds to form his patterns for a society and a state which are to correspond with the dignity of free and timeless spirits. It is, of course, unfortunate that no temporal reality can in fact correspond with the eternal Idea, since, as Plato already pointed out, 'seeing that everything that has a beginning has also an end, even a perfect Constitution such as yours will not last, but will, in time, be dissolved' (*Republic*). Still, we are free enough, though we were born in chains: we are in inalienable possession of eternal, changeless values which stand above the stream of Time, like the quiet moon reflecting its broken rays in the changing movement of the sea.

Actually, most philosophical interpretations of man's relation to Time can in the last analysis be summed up in two main tendencies: either to transfer *a priori* man's being into the Absolute, in which case it is impossible to take Time seriously: whence—*Alles Vergaengliche ist nur ein Gleichnis*; or else to make temporality consume human existence entirely, an attitude condemned on its own showing by ending in nihilism.

(c) *Futuristic Ideas of Time*

The latter view leads on, however, to the second answer to our original question as to the ultimate destiny of the temporal process. There are a great number of variations on this theme, and it is by no means easy to detect their fundamental similarity.

It is important to bear in mind that all the aspirations, failures and achievements of man are here visualized with re-

comparative lack of feeling for History, although, as we shall see presently, he had the great merit of having undermined once for all the Cartesian and Idealist claim to put Time into Space.

Man in Time

ference to a futurity which is the temporal sequence of the present age. The view may very well be cast in a pessimistic mould, as, for instance, in the cultural pessimism of Spengler, who was profoundly weary of the past and who believed that every civilization sets out and ends up with an experience of death. Moreover, if civilizations, as Spengler taught, are the counterparts of the seasons—spring, summer, autumn, and winter, we are driven into the vicious circle of perpetual recurrence for which Classicism is largely and fatally responsible. Other thinkers awaited the coming of a moment in Time when consciousness will be entirely extinct and life will fade away, and spoke contemptuously of History (Schopenhauer, Eduard Hartmann, Tolstoy). They were attended by a host of melodious *literati* who gave expression in their various ways to the once fashionable *taedium vitae*.

But the looking to the future assumed also optimistic forms. The confidence in the rational being of man, already characteristic in some measure of the ancient Classical philosophy of life, became the stimulus for an unheard of accumulation of knowledge, which enhanced man's hope in his victory over Nature. The pessimistic attitude of later Classical culture in regard to temporal reality was replaced by an outburst of historic optimism. This is true above all of the period of Enlightenment with its perfectionist interpretation of History and its growing power over everything except itself: more so than, as is commonly held, of the Renaissance, the period, that is to say, which divides the Middle Ages from so called Modern Times and in which there was as much decay and despair as hope and optimism.

The last three or four hundred years have been characterized by a whole series, more or less optimistic and perfectionist, of religious, philosophical, cultural and social trends and currents in which a common feeling for and experience of History (or lack of them) can be detected. Spell-bound by the triumph of man over Nature, they are, or most of them are, united by a tendency to degrade the interpretation of History to natural science, whereby historical events are treated in the same way as the 'objective facts' of physics or biology;[1] and by a strange unawareness of the truth that, as a great historian puts it, the

---

[1] See, e.g., the materialist Thomas Buckle (*History of Civilization*), one of the most interesting and extreme nineteenth-century representatives of this approach.

The End

student of History does not enter 'a world of animal nature, but a world which mankind has previously conquered by action, discovery, sacrifice, emotion' and that his facts 'are not facts in the common sense of this abused word: his facts are man's experiences'.[1] The historian, that is to say, is called upon to trace the secret threads, to expose the motives of men, to watch and read every emotion of hope and triumph, of terror and despair, till at last he reaches the hidden source, and origin, and end of human existence. And even if he must reckon with the growth of science, which is itself a fact of History (a fact, moreover, that has given man the terrible power of imperilling his very existence), this in no way implies falling into dependence on the sphere of those scientific presuppositions which attempt to tear man away from the ultimate sources of life. Indeed, the very destructiveness inherent in scientific knowledge and achievement compels us to transcend these presuppositions. Unfortunately various learned ignoramuses and professional historians still persist in wanting us to deal 'scientifically' with History, as if History can be detached from the sources of life and of men's awareness of them. Their purpose is to make a record of 'objective facts', that is to say, to relate exactly 'what was', and they reject in advance every kind of 'preconceived ideas which hamper the freedom of inquiry'. But they have a series of their own presuppositions, and, more often than not, rather tyrannical ones at that: above all they presuppose themselves and their 'presuppositionlessness' (if it may be permitted to coin a very long word). The first commandment of 'scientific thought', it would seem, runs: thou shalt emancipate thyself from all presuppositions! Descartes, who represents a milestone at the final end of the glorious thousand-year Night of the Middle Ages, a great turning-point with which modern history begins, was the first to proclaim this commandment unreservedly: there shall be no postulates in philosophy! *De omnibus dubitandum est.* Nevertheless, seeing that in actual fact we cannot do without postulates, even Descartes made at least one significant assumption, the assumption, namely, that Mystery should disappear from

[1] E. Rosenstock-Huessy, *Out of Revolution,* Autobiography of Western Man, p. 693; also the brilliant chapter 'Farewell to Descartes'. Prof. Arnold Toynbee says that the victory of laborious scientific and 'factual' method over historical thought (he calls it the 'industrialization' of historiography) is a *tour de force,* and the confidence of this victory 'the delusion of a false analogy' (*A Study of History,* vol. i, p. 4).

the purview of man. The truth, he asserts, is contained only in that which can be recognized 'clearly and distinctly'. This assumption was not and could not be subject to any doubt, whether of God or of man. . . . We, on the contrary, venture to state at this early stage of our inquiry that we desire no 'clarity' or 'distinction': *et qu'on ne nous reproche pas la manque de clarté, car nous en faisons profession* (Pascal). We must and shall do what philosophers and scientists persistently refuse to do: we must 'laugh, weep, and hate', rather than be 'objective', else our search will avail nothing.

One may distinguish three tendencies in the optimistic hope in futurity. In the first place, the Anglo-Saxon school, which awaits salvation from some new Constitution of a commonwealth that would secure the life of individuals and of states and remove all the frictions and contradictions characteristic of the present order of things. 'If the human species is given time it will always act wisely' (Burke). The realization of the British Commonwealth of nations guided by the rule of law and public spirit is in itself a forward step towards a new form of existence. The hope which inspired the evolutionary philosophy of a Herbert Spencer is that History will be fulfilled in the end by the bringing into existence of a prosperous and leisured world in a future utopia, even though it may be impossible now for men to reach the promised land. Thus History tends to lose its transcendent dimensions altogether. The ideals (or idols) of Natural Law and the Law of Reason invest men with the claim to bring about the fulfilment of History. Philosophy itself becomes synonymous with practical ethics, as in Bentham, Mill, Spencer and others. Time is regarded as a mere succession of indivisible moments, just as Space consists of indivisible points (Locke, Hume), and Eternity is a mere repetition of finite ideas.[1]

The other tendency is of French origin: it was principally represented by Rousseau and Saint-Simon, whose philosophy is the germ-cell of a multitude of the later theories about future destiny, such as that of Comte (with his formula 'order and progress'), Marx (who, however, occupies a special position and whose immense contribution to the understanding of man in

---

[1] See Locke's significant statement about the idea we have of God: 'If I find that I know some few things, I can frame an idea of knowing twice as many; the same may also be done of the duration of existence without beginning or end, and so I frame the idea of an eternal being' (*Essay* II, c. 23).

History will be discussed later on), as well as the ideologies of various social democracies. They were all under the spell of the English empiricists and tried to persuade mankind that they could alter the course of the world by a man-made theory. Henceforth Time and History were deemed a kind of intellectual machinery of means and ends rather than a living destiny. The motto which Saint-Simon put over his philosophy—the Golden Age is coming!—implied that all the suffering, and toil, and tragedy of the present is a means to the coming future and is outweighed and made worth while by the final objective in Time. Undoubtedly, there was an experience at the basis of this attitude which could not but be an instinctive survival of the Christian virtue of hope, of *amor futuri*, of the vision of human brotherhood and the linking up of all generations in Christ: in fact, a secular form of the mysteries of the Kingdom of God. This applies equally, and even to a greater extent, to the Anglo-Saxon school, since in England 'social progress' has hardly, as on the European Continent, been associated with Rationalism but, on the contrary, was largely inspired by Christian consciousness. Nevertheless, the natural development was erroneously believed to lead by itself straight into God's Kingdom, even though, unlike in Stoicism, the world was not taken as one finds it but was to be recast and transformed. The Declaration of the Rights of Man in the French Revolution was regarded as the first step toward the coming of the Golden Age; the rise of Industry—a possible further step on the same road.

A similar position is occupied by the so-called Religious-Historical school which professed a futurism side by side with a belief in the survival of the 'evolving' human soul. Ernst Troeltsch, one of the main representatives of this school, to whose views we shall return later in another context, suggested (despite his loyalty to Lutheranism and his belief that medieval Catholicism is a deviation from 'the Gospel') that the traditional myths of the Church about the final destiny of men should be replaced by Dante's *Divina Commedia*, which expresses the supreme ethical ideal as a development ascending from the values of the life of this world to those of the transcendent realm. He believed, therefore, the *Commedia* to be the greatest eschatological witness of Christendom. He expected a continuous development reaching out into the beyond and thus fulfilling its aim. Through knowledge of the self-destructive effects of evil,

through the pain of purification, human souls would draw near to God. And the union of all souls in divine love would lead to a final absorption of men in God. A similar approach can be detected in the various constructions of Anthroposophy in which transmigrations and reincarnations are regarded as means to a gradual ascension of the soul and its final attainment of a state of supreme perfection.

Futurism had been possible only because of the underlying conception and experience of Time as a stream flowing equably along. The past is essentially the same as the present and the future: nothing really occurs in Time in the sense of new *events* invading its gradual course; and History presents itself as a wholly rational and predictable process.

Yet Marx had already little confidence in the goodness and altruism of the human individual, who needed only to be freed from artificial restraints and to be set in a Nature similarly liberated, for him to arrive at the gates of paradise, and he handed over the establishment of the future Kingdom to the proletariat which had nothing to lose except its chains. His conception of Time was no more based on the idea of mere perfection as removed to some future stage of evolution: the famous Marxist dialectic is in fact inconceivable without the discovery of the illogical, tragic and revolutionary possibilities of History from which the Rousseaus and Voltaires and Saint-Simons were as widely removed as possible.

We have now arrived at a point of transition. Instead of an ordered evolution man foresees a catastrophe, in which the present world would perish and a new one arise upon its ashes. As in the varied and colourful images of biblical apocalypticism there emerges a picture of things to come which are the continuation of the present order, but in a radically revised and improved edition.[1] But even this trend of thought was not a real variance with the 'futurism' which underlies all these attitudes and in which the problem of Time has in the last resort remained beyond the purview of man: it has taken Time more or less naïvely for granted, be it by way of historical

[1] There is no doubt that Marxism bears the marks of origin from the apocalyptic and messianic faith of Israel, besides being inspired by an echo of Christian universalism; but in a tremendous act of substitution the Proletariat has taken the place of the Chosen People. The messianic Kingdom of Marx is however by no means a merely material Kingdom, since it is to be revealed by an act of creation: *Im Anfang war die Tat!*

The End

pessimism or optimism, with or without biblical background and belief in immortality; and in all these cases we are confronted with a mind that tends to ignore the transcendent and truly apocalyptic dimensions of Time.

We are compelled to question the very premise, the whole 'either-or', on which these views rest, the conception, that is, of a self-relying temporality in which we can safely proceed in our various movements or from which we can escape into a supra-temporal sphere, as in Greek and Idealist thought.

Chapter III

THE CONTRADICTIONS OF TIME

The first sign of a wholly different approach to the problem under discussion goes rather far back and can be seen in the important transitional period between the prophets of the Old Testament and the New Testament world of ideas, that is, the later Jewish apocalypticism: Time itself is something that must be transcended. Instead of the futuristic expectation of a Kingdom of God on earth there appears the distinction, in imagery that may still be derived from futuristic ideas, of two aeons (*olam hasse* and *olam hobbah*), wholly different and yet interrelated.[1] And the question inevitably arises whether Time is not a reality that acquires meaning from beyond itself, while, coterminously, Meaning cannot be apprehended outside the to-and-fro movements of Time. In our own days this question has acquired new significance. . . . There are thoughts and insights, it would appear, which pervade the air of certain times, arising independently in the minds of men belonging to the same age or calling to one another across the ages. Many minds believe that all the riddles of life are resumed in the mystery of Time and that, should we know what Time really is, we may be able to resolve all the perplexities of human existence.

Bergson, in his *Essai sur les données immédiates de la conscience*, endeavoured to solve the most difficult philosophical problem, that of freedom, from the point of view of a new interpretation of temporal duration (durée réelle) and Spengler followed in his footsteps, without however being directly dependent on him. The recent phenomenological inquiries of Heidegger into the nature of Time, Einstein's relativization of the Time-measure,

[1] See M. J. Lagrange, *Le Messianisme chez les Juifs*, and Martin Buber, *Das Koenigtum Israels*, both of whom tend to regard this distinction underlying the idea of transcendence of God's Kingdom as implicit in Jewish monotheism from the very beginning. See also Christopher North's illuminating book *The Old Testament Interpretation of History*.

The End

Minkovsky's discovery of a 'fourth dimension' in Time, as well as Milne's new theories which claim that, though indistinguishable on the empirical scale, there are two different measures of Time leading to different cosmologies—all these point in the same direction and give the lie to physicists, who used to believe that they knew exactly what they were doing when they measured time-intervals, and could afford to despise the speculations of the philosophers and theologians about the nature of Time. This new awareness of Time, though perhaps still in search of adequate articulation, has yet revealed one very important and fundamental truth: it has eliminated the parallelism between Time and (mathematical) Space.

Kant, as we saw, had established the categories of time and space as the two correlative forms (*Denkformen*) for the perception of the world of phenomena: the line in time corresponds to the line in space. The one is measured by seconds, the other by yards. But Bergson showed how misleading this is. The apparent similarity between the two rests on the erroneous belief that we are able to measure Time with a watch in our hand, just as we can measure space with a yardstick. Are we really measuring Time when using a chronometer to establish, for instance, how many hours a car takes to go from London to Oxford? In point of fact we have merely established that two mechanical occurrences in space, i.e. the course of the clock and the running of the car are related to each other in such a way as to show that certain elements of one occurrence correspond to certain elements of the other. In other words we merely state the simultaneity between the duration of two processes. The duration itself, however, i.e., real Time, has not even been approached by this method of measuring. This is clarified by a further example. Supposing our watch, as well as the car, ran a thousand times faster and the tempo of all the other happenings were accelerated in an equal measure: in that case none of our instruments would enable us even to notice the acceleration. Time itself, *durée réelle*, the constant flux of instants is, therefore, wholly beyond the range of these instruments.[1]

But if that be so, how can, and do, we apprehend Time?

[1] It is interesting to contrast the mechanical measuring of Time by clocks, or calendars, or astronomical statistics with the way in which the profound mythological language of the Bible speaks of it, where the 'days' of creation are constituted by what and how God deals with man and man with God—events which, in the end, take all the time of History.

The Contradictions of Time

There appears to be but one answer to the question: Time can only be *experienced*. The 'duration' of Time is not something that imposes itself upon us extraneously through the medium of objective observation. Time is the category of our very being and existence. *In te, anima mea, tempora metior* (St. Augustine).

If, then, Time is not a measurable self-contained entity, but the form of our very existence, not to be perceived in any objectified manner, we are again confronted with the central issue in the understanding of man's temporal existence, the question, namely, whether our life on the scale of external things and objects is all that we have to be concerned with, or whether it points to another dimension which transcends Time and is yet vitally related to it. In other words, can we escape the seemingly issueless eschatological dilemma: return into a supratemporal sphere with its attendant depotentiation of Time, oblivion of the worldly course of events or heavenly egotism on the one hand, and optimistic or pessimistic evolutionism, utopianism and 'catastrophic end-spectacles' on the other?

(a) Implicatissimum Aenigma

God created Time. Such is our assumption, and we shall attempt to show its far-reaching implications. We renounce the approach which begins with the abstract terms of Eternity and Time, of absolute and contingent being, of substance and phenomenon, standing in a relation of opposition, co-ordination or subordination to each other, but set out with the triune realm of God, Time and History—the three realities by which or in which man lives and has his being. God created Time, and all that he created, is created as being in Time. Nothing and nobody can be known by being taken out of Time. Neither can man know himself by extracting himself from out of Time. His subjective feeling for Time may change: he may resist it or eject it altogether. Yet his existence will remain existence in Time, of whose reality he cannot but be more or less intensely conscious.

There is probably one, and only one, thinker who has presented the problem of Time in all its profundity: it is St. Augustine (see *Confessions*, xi, 9–31; *De civitate Dei*, xii); and though we shall have to oppose this great Christian teacher on other issues

where, as we believe, he has betrayed the original Christian vision, we cannot fail to realize his amazing insight into the mystery of Time.

Time, being created by God, is not a human concept, nor a rational '*a priori*', but a mysterious reality whose true nature is beyond the faculties of ratiocination. Si nemo ex me quaerat, scio: si quaerenti explicari velim, nescio (if no one questions me, I know: if I would explain to a questioner, I know not, *Conf.*, xi, 14). The seemingly self-evident is revealed as being, in fact, an absolute enigma. The most ordinary fact signifies a secret to which God alone has access. Time is the *implicatissimum aenigma*. The future is not yet. The past is no more. The present has no extension: it is Time only in as much as it elapses into the past. And yet Time *is*. It has no beginning nor end. And yet it must of necessity and by its very nature be somehow limited. It does not endure; and yet we appear to measure it. Thus the dictum 'man lives in Time' signifies above everything else: man lives in an impenetrable mystery.

We do not dispose of the order of Time with either our thought or our very existence. We are thrown into fast flowing, never resting Time, streaming irresistibly from future into past. There is nothing in us that does not fall under the force of this torrential movement. We have no power to bring it to a standstill or to extract ourselves from it. Time is not known as the movement of the sun, the moon or the stellar bodies, rather, it is the movement of our very being. Dies transeunt, et quomodo nescio. It seizes and carries man off into the waste of the desultory and passing *Now*, into perpetual disquiet. Ego in tempora dissilui, quorum ordinem nescio, et tumultuosis varietatibus dilaniniantur cogitationes meae, intima viscera animae meae. . . . (I have been severed amid times, whose order I know not; and my thoughts, even the inmost bowels of my soul, are rent and mangled with tumultuous varieties, *Conf.*, xi, 29). The numberless, fleeting moments cast man into the flood of temporality, and every moment emerges as a wholly new, never to be repeated, never such as it has been. Time creates perpetually new situations which rush upon us, which we cannot escape, which plunge us into anxiety, into questioning, into haste, into restless or joyous expectation, or oppressive and exacting memories. Time brings disquiet and demonic need for perpetual progression. Man cannot afford to rest, be it through the won-

The Contradictions of Time

derful ministry of memory whereby he seeks to preserve as a
constant present the image of the past, but which lapses irresistibly into a lurid darkness, or through mysterious presenti-
ments whereby he tries to gaze into the unknown future (*Conf.*,
x, 9). Both turn into illusions and the chain of Time cannot ever
be torn asunder.[1]

But even more: we come to know the terrible finitude of
human life, the final possibility of which is death. From its
first instant human existence is a relentless drawing towards
death: ut omnino nihil aliud tempus vitae huius, quam cursus
ad mortem. In a year I shall be nearer death than a year before,
to-morrow nearer than to-day. . . . We are far away here from
the Idealist or Cartesian metaphysics, which lead man's mind
beyond the all-too-real, dooming reality of death. Nobody can
arrest or retard the deadly course—this strange and terrible
danse macabre, which overtakes all things, even the 'eternal' laws
of logic: twice two=nought! All haste *pari motu* towards death
and carry its seeds within them. Man's very existence is *tempus
in morte*. Numquam igitur in vita homo est. All things that are in
Time pass away: and though they arise, become, grow and
reach their maturity, yet even thus they reveal the beginning of
decay and death. . . . The 'healthy' human being, who lives life
'fully' may well forget death or not believe in it: he knows *of*
death, but he does not know *death*. Only in rare lightning instants, he suddenly remembers, sees death face to face, aware
of its presence from within, as if he were actually dying: and
such seeing is already a realization of other dimensions, a witness, coming from the deep, of there being an End.

So far we seem to hear the same voice as that of Dilthey or
Nietzsche. In point of fact there is a fundamental difference
between these voices. Whereas the latter calls on man to command an abstract view of the phenomenon of Time or else
makes him a victim of Time's corruptibility, the former testifies
to Time, in all its agony, as acquiring meaning in self-transcendence which is at once its surpassing and its affirmation: in other

---

[1] Cf. Anna Comnena's version of the motto of nearly all histories by
Byzantine authors: 'Time, flowing unrestrainably and always on the move,
carries away and carries off all things that come into being and engulfs
them in the deep sea of oblivion, whether they be things not worth a song
or things great and memorable. In the language of Tragedy, Time bringeth
what was not to birth, and as for that which hath seen Light, lo, Time
shroudeth it and it is gone' (quoted by Arnold Toynbee, op. cit.).

The End

words, an attitude grounded in the fact of God's revelation in Time, in the Christian myth, which is also the Christian fact, of *God-manhood*.[1] Time cannot be known from within Time alone, since the inherent structure of Time is that it reveals a precipitate movement from future into past, and we, who attempt to grasp it, are existentially involved in that movement: whence all understanding within this movement can be but 'relative' (Dilthey) or 'perspective' (Nietzsche). The *proton pseudos*, the fundamental error, of the philosophers, however, lies in that they tend to commit a Christological heresy, that is, to dissect the mystery of God-manhood: they separate God and Time either by severing God from man and putting themselves in the place of God, or by dividing man from God; by failing to see that God created Time 'in the beginning', that 'when the fulness of Time came, God sent forth His Son', and that 'he will be revealed in his Time'. In the power of God-manhood there can be no cleavage nor confusion between the realm of Time and that which transcends Time, since the latter is entering Time and Time, in its very corruptibility, presses towards self-transcendence. And though God is beyond all Time, he is yet related to it: he acts with and in the movements of Time, and all things occur and are according to their unique divine-human situation.

The decisive question is What enables man to find his way beyond 'enigmatic' Time by which his existence is bounded? How can he overcome the disquiet, the pain, the transitoriness and apparent godlessness of Time and find the peace of eternal life? *Koennt ich zum Augenblicke sagen: Verweile Augenblick, du bist so schoen!* (Faust). Is there a final vision of a peaceful earth, even if all the ages between to-day and the end are perpetual disruption, struggle, agony and war?

Before turning to see if and how these and such like questions can be answered, we must discuss some important points in the philosophical understanding of Time, which should, moreover,

---

[1] The subject of God-manhood will be discussed more fully at a later stage. . . . I shall not enter here into a discussion of the question-begging identification of 'myth' and 'fact'. What is a myth? A mere tale, a lie, a fairy story for adults? No, it is the very garb of History. Only the 'lower truths', as Plato already perceived, 'walk about naked'; the 'higher truths' are robed in myths, so that truth may be seen through 'fable', as the body is seen through the woven tissue: the sacred is vested in the profane—a paradox that no Aristotle has ever been capable of comprehending.

enable us to see more clearly the conclusions to which St. Augustine's analysis have brought us.

(b) The Kantian Antinomy

Kant had raised the important issue as to whether it is not an altogether unrealizable thought, a *contradictio in adjecto*, to speak of a 'fulfilment' in Time. Is not every end of Time also a moment in Time, i.e. another beginning and, therefore, a continuation of the temporal line? And this question has a corollary, namely, whether it is possible at all to conceive of a time-interval without being involved in contradictions?

Bearing in mind Kant's statement, though not necessarily his solution, of the antinomy of Time, we are confronted with two mutually contradictory propositions, each of which can apparently be proved: (a) Time has *no* beginning or end, since every beginning must be the end of a preceding time, and every end the beginning of a time to come; (b) Time *has* a beginning and an end, else every present moment could be the duration of a whole eternity, which, it would seem, does not make sense, since Eternity is not a duration and cannot be limited as regards Time (or Space). One may argue furthermore that if Time has no beginning or end, then the present moment A would be the termination of an infinitely long time. Equally, the moment B which terminates the next hour would be the end of an infinitely long time. Consequently, the temporal stretch terminating with A would be as infinite as the stretch terminating with B. A part would therefore be equal to the whole, which, logically speaking, does not make sense. We must conclude, therefore, that every attempt to conceive Time inevitably leads to two views which bear in themselves manifest contradictions. It is quite naïve to assume that a beginningless and endless Time is a valid concept, while the concept of a beginning and ending Time is meaningless and contradictory. We cannot get away from the fact that no stretch of Time can be conceived of without a proceeding, progressing, forward-going *Now*: and progress from one point to the other presupposes an ultimate point of direction or orientation toward which we proceed or from which we recede.

The fact of Time confronts us with the same sort of difficulty which is involved in thinking of our birth or death, of the waking

The End

or the extinction of consciousness. How can my consciousness have begun or how can it cease, since the points of the beginning and the end of consciousness must alike lie within the purview of consciousness itself? I must have experienced, or I shall have to experience, this moment. And if I do so it can no longer be the beginning or the end of consciousness, because my consciousness cannot experience such moments except as points of transition from one state to another. And yet, despite these contradictions, we do in fact experience the waking and the extinction of consciousness.

Kant, as is known, tried to resolve the difficulty epistemologically by showing that both statements about Time are equally false and answer a wrongly put question. They are, according to him, based on a confusion of the 'thing in itself' and the world of 'appearance'. But this can hardly be recognized as a solution of the problem of Time. The very fact that Kant appears to have found rest and peace for his mind in this solution is a sign of his not having perceived and experienced the inescapable terror and tragedy of Time, as St. Augustine did and as we do, whether we want to or not.

Granted that Time is a form of perception, the question still remains: can this form of perception be transcended, or does it remain a fixed, immutable category of thought? Can the chains of Time be broken? Can Time 'end', be 'redeemed', integrated into something that overcomes its spell-bound movement? And if this were possible, are we not met, again and again, with the apparently meaningless proposition of a temporal end of temporality? Or does Time continue *ad infinitum*, in which case there can be no *process* in Time, because such a process is conceivable only as approximation to or recession from a point of orientation in Time?

It appears, then, that we are compelled to decide between the two answers to the question of the end of all things. Either Time remains untranscendable, and cannot be overcome except by escaping into a supra-temporal and non-temporal sphere; or else it can and must be overcome by relating it to its End. We cannot avoid the decision by way of the Kantian distinction of 'thing in itself' and 'phenomena'. As a matter of fact we cannot decide either way while relying on mere ratiocination: reason demands the rejection of both solutions. But the decision can be made on 'existential' grounds, on the grounds of the mutual

relation of God and man; and the language in which we speak must necessarily be mythological.

(c) *God in Time*

When speaking of God's relation to Time we must bear in mind that God can manifest himself only indirectly in Time. He cannot be objectified in Time, though Time is the realm of his revelation. The existence of God can be (and in some sense must be) denied. The contradictions in which we were involved when attempting to think of Time signify that it bears within itself something utterly irrational, insoluble, unless indeed it can find its fulfilment beyond itself. If God *is* and Time is what it is, then Time must be capable of transcending itself, of revealing its hidden transcendent meaning. Such a *fulfilment* of Time is the only possible answer to the Kantian problem. We do not dispose of this fulfilment, although our existence is what it is, and ought to be, only in relation to it. It is God's doing, and it is our doing only in so far as God does it. The two sides of the antinomy epitomize the tension in which our faith in God perceives the mystery of Time. The one pole of the antinomy, the fact, that is to say, that Time must have a beginning and an end corresponds to our awareness that Time is not something eternal *in itself*, or something that will 'endure' for ever. The other pole, however, the fact, that is to say, that Time is infinite, expresses our strange certainty about the eternal meaning and content of Time; in other words, the fact that to transcend Time is not to annul it, but to redeem it and to reveal its true potentiality, of which History is already a realization (see below). If God does not disclose himself in Time, he is no God. It is not sufficient, indeed it is a falsehood, to suggest that God has merely enabled us to escape the present age in a Platonic way, since this would only make absolute the issueless and deadly curse of Time. But is man's destiny a mere survival after death, a liberation whereby the 'immortal animal' receives a higher state, while his mortal life can be safely put away as empty and devoid of meaning? Or is the gateway to eternal life a *resurrection*—Eternity through Time, victory through defeat, joy through sorrow, life (not ghostly survival) restored and glorified through and by death? Does not the reconciliation of the contradictions of Time lie in that God's relation to it is not a jump

into the void, but is grounded in love, in that God *is* love, in the power of which the God-Man, the Son of God who is the Son of Man, suffers and dies and succumbs under the mortal course of Time in order to redeem Time, to rise and reign for ever? If there is a victory over the last enemy, which is death, then we must be prepared to comprehend the truth contained in this question, even though it appears to us as contradictory as death itself. The deadly ambiguities of Time cry out for an answer beyond its own limits: it aspires at each and every point towards a moment where it is coincidentally transcended and fulfilled. This moment is, as it were, a final point in Time if seen from one angle, and it is Eternity if seen from another.

To return, now, to St. Augustine's analysis, we must conclude that man alone has no power to acquire peace, since he is existentially bound up with the flux of Time. The cry of God Incarnate from the cross: my God, my God, why hast thou forsaken me?—gives the lie to all the heroic philosophies of transcendentalism in which we are supposed to find peace and comfort to our minds. Man's creatureliness, that is, his very relation to God and God's relation to him, is existence in Time, and peace is given to man through the final leap into the beyond which does not annul Time but fulfils it. Facis et visiones temporales et ipsa tempora et quietatem ex tempore (Thou makest things seen in Time, yea the Times themselves, and the rest which results from Time, *Conf.*, xiii, 37).

Thus, with all the contradictions involved, Time is yet profoundly meaningful: it can and does become the realm of divine and human purpose. Indeed, we may say with Nietzsche's Zarathustra against all attempts to deny Time, be it in its mortal anguish or in its hidden promise: 'Evil I declare, and hostile to mankind—this doctrine of the One, the Perfect, the Unmoved, the Sufficient, the Intransitory. The Intransitory!—it's but a simile—and the poets lie exceedingly. But the best images shall speak of Time and Becoming; they shall be for praise and justification of all transitoriness!'

'When the fulness of Time came, God sent forth his Son' (Gal. iv, 4.), the Mediator 'betwixt thee, the One, and us many . . . that by him I may apprehend in whom I have been apprehended' (*Conf.* xi, 29; see Phil. iii, 12–14). The Word became flesh. God came into Time and took Time upon himself. Christ revealed the crucial point in Time, the *End* of Time, there-

The Contradictions of Time

by affecting our whole experience and understanding of Time. True, the stream of Time continues to flow in its restless movement from future into past, in turmoil, pain and constant changeableness. And man goes on existing in this perpetual flux. But this very flux brings man to a point where a new dimension is revealed to him, where God himself is engaged in his existence: in the power of a divine-human event Time acquires meaning—a meaning, not a logically evident rationality. The process of Time does not inspire much by deduction, but it does so by insight into its divine-human significance, which exhibits at once its tragedy and promise, and has the power to make that promise realize itself, a power to make it the transcendent ground and fulfilment of temporality.

God becomes, as it were, the inmost component of events, throwing his light and shadow on the things and relations of the present age, albeit this indwelling remains still hidden and ambiguous to us. *That is what renders Time History, for History is Time which has acquired meaning within itself through having transcended itself;* and the prime reality of Time transcending itself and thus acquiring meaning is revealed in Christ, the God-Man.

Chapter IV

THE END

Since the very contradictions of Time point to Christ and in him find their resolution, we must now try to analyse more closely what the End really signifies from the Christian point of view. What is the New Testament view of the End τὸ τέλος? *Telos* means fulfilment in which all temporality is transmuted, that is to say, not obliterated or destroyed but fulfilled. The End is conceived, on the one hand, as a kind of temporal term, as it were, a third act in Time's drama: '*then* (cometh) the end' (εἶτα τὸ τέλος, 1 Cor. xv, 24,) which is preceded by 'Christ the *first fruits*' (ἀπαρχὴ Χριστός), and '*afterward* that are Christ's' (ἔπειτα οἱ Χριστοῦ).[1] But, on the other hand, this temporal end is eternal—a transcending of the very category of Time and all 'the fashion of this world' (σχῆμα τοῦ κόσμου τούτου 1 Cor. vii, 31).

Without further scrutinizing the details of this New Testament thought, let us refer it back to its premise. The disintegrating forces of Time subvert the creature which has lost its immediate relation to God. But as creature it still preserves this relation in some sense, since its very creaturehood reveals that relation. Its fall is a token of its greatness—which is true of man in his demonic self-assertion over against God as much as of Lucifer, the 'Son of the Morning'. 'The earth is the Lord's, and the fulness thereof.' Both terms 'fallen' and 'creation'—must retain their equal force and validity. Only thus arises the peculiar tension as well as the balance of man's predicament as expressed in the biblical witness.[2] The fact that we exist in a divided world

---

[1] Cf. also 2 Cor. v, 4: 'For we that are in this tabernacle do groan, being burdened: not for that we should be unclothed, but clothed upon, that mortality might be swallowed up of Life.'

[2] This is shown with reference to man in the important patristic distinction between the divine 'image' and 'similitude' in man, which no efforts of modern theologians, however ingenious, have been able to destroy.

is evidenced above all in the following antinomy: God is present; he is the ground of all things. Yet he remains invisible; he is beyond man's reach; indeed, he can be denied. 'Faith is the evidence of things *not seen*.' And God's presence is realized 'in the Spirit'—the medium by which man within Time is yet beyond it, within the 'Kingdom of God'.[1] God cannot be objectified; he is not a thing side by side with, or over against, other things accessible to our empirical perception. The moment we attempt to think of God in terms of things and objects, we are inevitably reducing him to an idol. It is impossible, therefore, to express the relation between Time and God except in painful tension. Since, however, God is the ground of life and of all things, every temporal reality, every element in History and Nature, and all the relations pertaining to the present age become transcendently meaningful. All temporal realities have a depth: they are, in the words of St. Irenaeus *istorika pneumatikos*, while divine things are made real in Time and History: *pneumatika istorikos*.[2] But the divine content of creaturely existence is, as it were, imprisoned and enchained: it is, to use a physical analogy which may well be an irony to-day, like atoms which contain immense power but which we are (or were!) unable to split in order to free the hidden forces. The treasure is mysteriously shrouded and concealed. Is it possible to demonstrate God's presence or, indeed, to prove his existence? Does belief in God rest on a traceable providence? What is God's own theodicy, God's final self-justification to the world? These questions which we shall discuss later on, press in upon us from behind the great enigma of Time. We are all too prone to transfer to the

[1] This is one of the principle themes of Johannine theology which is in keeping with the old Jewish conception of the 'Spirit of God' as the 'Presence' (*shekinah*) of God in the world.

[2] The familiar view that the Eastern Fathers were lacking in a sense of History is founded on next to nothing. Henri de Lubac, whose profound patristic knowledge is exhibited in his remarkable book *Catholicisme*, writes quoting Gregory of Nyssa and Maximus the Confessor respectively: 'Tous les pères veulent "comprendre l'esprit de l'histoire, sans en ébranler la réalité historique" (*Contra Eunomium*). Car—c'est un grec, et l'un des moins "historistes", qui nous le dit—il y a une "force spirituelle" de l'histoire (*Quaestiones ad Thalassium*); par leur finalité, les faits eux-mêmes ont un dedans; ils sont déjà, dans le temps, chargés de l'éternité. Et en revanche, la réalité . . . n'est pas seulement spirituelle, mais incarnée. . . . Car le Verbe se fait chair, et il plante sa tente au milieu de nous. Le sens spirituelle est donc répandu partout . . . et d'abord et essentiellement dans la réalité elle-même.' (p. 122.)

transcendent sphere that quality of reality which denotes our divided empirical existence. We often treat God as if he were a kind of magnified penny-in-the-slot machine full of goods to provide for the various needs of men, and we expect God to comply with our intellectual, emotional and sensible perceptions if he is to be the 'object' of our recognition. Hence the fierce and largely pointless controversy which rages between those who seek to prove the existence of God and those who would deny it. Hence also the evil propensity shown by men struggling to secure the omnipotence of and subordination to God and to defy God in the strength of the plea of proving, or protecting, or defending him.

What, then, are we to say of *telos*? It is not a 'special' fact apart from other facts, a 'special' manifestation apart from others, a 'supernatural' miracle above and outside 'nature'; it is not the creation of a new 'thing' next to and over against old 'things', but rather the disclosure of a hidden content of Time: in other words apocalypse. Both familiar statements, therefore 'the End is coming' and 'the End is already here' (i.e. concealed and yet present in the power of God-manhood) are true; and the more apart they appear, the more needful they are to one another. The way to the End is in the End itself.

There is a tendency in biblical theology to oppose or juxtapose St. Paul's allegedly exclusive Jewish eschatology of two worlds or ages, on the one hand, the present one to be ended and the next one to be brought about by a catastrophic act of God and a universal judgment, and, on the other hand, St. John's supposedly exclusive Hellenic cosmology, in which the contrast between present and future worlds is merged in the contrast between the evil world which passes away and the eternal truth of God which is revealed in Christ in the darkness of the present world. [1] Actually both visions are equally true: they are two co-inherent sides of a single reality. And, significantly enough, St. Paul himself has shown that no temporal line can in fact be drawn between this world and the next (of which the risen manhood of Christ is already the realization or the first-fruit), [2] while St. John too speaks of the 'last day' as a historical or

---

[1] The findings of recent biblical studies, however, have shown conclusively that no such opposition is in fact warranted by the authentic biblical witness. See, e.g., C. H. Dodd, *The Apostolic Teaching*.

[2] See the passage quoted above; also Eph. ii, 6: 'God *has* raised us up together, and made us sit together in heavenly places in Christ Jesus.'

The End

quasi-historical event, which is still in the future.[1] No one, indeed, has attained such a true vision of abiding divine presence and historical fulfilment as St. John.

(a) Time and History

We have said that History is Time acquiring meaning. This may well sound a mockery in an age when we are witnessing not only the destructive forces of Time (for we always have to pay the price of Time with our very existence) but a judgment upon History itself and its power over the brain and heart of men. How can we speak of History as Meaning, seeing that we are thrown into the midst of untold historic turmoils and confusions which periodically spew out their human victims? May it not be that, in the words of Joyce's *Ulysses*, 'History is the nightmare from which I shall awake,' being, as it is apparently, a truceless war with man? And yet we cannot avoid the distinction of Time and History, and we cannot identify the two. All things, the whole animate and inanimate world, are in Time. Only man is a being of History, and only human destiny can be properly described as historical. It is this that marks the difference between the philosophy of History and mere scientific knowledge, because the former is concerned with seeing life from the point of view of man or, rather, in and through man, a historical being and thus related to God, to other men and to Nature; while science deals with objects outside of History and hence not only apart from God but also apart from man. This is true even of such sciences as biology, psychology and sociology, which view man as alienated from Reality and interpret him in terms of thinghood, that is to say, as a thing existing side by side with other things in a divided world.

History is no mere 'fact' or 'datum', or series of 'facts' and 'data', but above everything else a call, a vocation, a dispensation to be heard and responded to by free human beings—in short, the interaction of God and man. And it is this that makes man ask about his historical predicament. There can, therefore, be nothing fixed and immutable about the meaningfulness of Time and History. History is indeed pregnant with meaning; yet there is nothing 'lawful' or 'reasonable' about it. Contrary to the view of some, it cannot be conceived in terms of cause and

[1] See 1 John ii, 18; also John v, 20-29.

effect, and it stands beyond the immutable laws of Nature as
science knows her.[1] History cannot be confined to the sequence
of natural causes; it cannot be deduced; it is not even primarily
something that is remembered and recorded ('the great dust-
heap called "history" '), as the common definition of History
seems to suggest. Causality is a category which can be applied
to the world of objects and things, of properties and mechanical
relations only, whereas human existence, with all its tormenting
inward riddles, is not the working of a cause but a *destiny*: events
occur, happenings are caused.[2] And he who approaches History
with the categories of cause and effect or of law and evolution
will find 'data' or predetermined facts rather than life, or grace,
or freedom, or providence—rather, in other words, than the
eventful, the unforeseen, the incalculable, even if, no doubt, inwardly motivated; rather, in short, than all that which is the
pre-eminent hallmark of History.

One cannot insist too much or too often on the now familiar
assertion that History is not a gradual progress or an expanding
evolution, an idea by which some minds, however, still seem to
be intoxicated. History is not an ordered movement, and there
are no signs whatever that it is so. One need not be a Spenglerian to acknowledge that History presents not only a vast field
of battle, tragic collision and despair, but that historic movements, cultures and civilizations appear to die in their own
dialectic and become stupefied by their own surfeit. But this
cannot be regarded as a source of peculiar satisfaction, of *Schad-
enfreude*, as has become customary with certain contemporary
theologians, philosophers and sociologists in prophetic garb,
who rationalize their disillusions and apparently derive pleasure
from such rationalization: the destruction of Sodom and Gomor-
rah is not something to be gazed at from outside, and he who
does so will turn into a pillar of salt. The repudiation of evolu-

---

[1] C. B. Vico, for example, being under the impression of the apparent
lawfulness prevailing in the natural sciences, contended that historical
events also follow each other according to unswerving natural laws. The
Encyclopedists and Saint-Simon shared this view. This led to an outlook
in which man was seen as completely immersed, and driven on, by the
current extraneous tendencies, so that Auguste Comte could speak of an
'*histoirc sans noms*' (or, we may add, '*sans hommes*', which is the same
thing).

[2] Cf. the lines of T. S. Eliot:
*All that I could hope to make you understand
Is only events: not what has happened.*

tionism does not prevent us, moreover, from seeing the glory of God in things as they are, blinking nothing of the terror and yet sure of the Kingdom of God with all our mind and heart. But we are unable to detect any 'self-realizing Idea of humanity', in the face of which all particular events in the movement of History are believed to withdraw into the background or, still more, to become irrelevant. The Hegelian conception of History as a progressively realized objectification of a divine Idea, as the teleological working out of immanent Mind which controls the contents of historical experience and gradually eliminates what is negative in them; the old mechanistic views of evolution in which the course of events is dealt with as determined by the past; or the more recent views of 'emergent evolution' with its 'life-forces' and 'unconscious struggles to overcome limitation' *à la* Huxley, Alexander, Wells or Shaw; or for the matter of that, the pessimistic evolutionism which denies any issue for the confused ways of the world and puts man's trust in the generalities of systematic dissolution—all these generate laws and principles but do not interpret History: they supplant the living logic of historical events by mechanics in metaphysical or physiological garb. It is worse still when these views are interpolated into Christianity and lead men to 'apply' a thus diluted Christianity to a shattered world.[1] In the face of all this we are prepared to say with Nietzsche (*Before Sunrise*): '*Von Ungefaehr* (by chance)—that is the oldest title of nobility in the world, and I restore it to all things. I redeem them from their enslavement to things. This freedom of heavenly certainty I set like an azure bell over all things, when I taught them that . . . in them there is no "eternal will" . . . when I taught them that one thing at least is impossible—rationality. A little reason, doubtless, a seed of wisdom, scattered from star to star . . . this leaven is mingled

---

[1] To take just one example among a multitude of others, read the reassuring solemnity in Griffith-Jones's *Providence—Divine and Human*: 'it ("holy Love", or, as he terms it elsewhere, "epigenetic evolution"!) is stimulative of hope that, in spite of the sad facts of life and instability of progress, if only man joins his forces to those of the divine purpose, the best is yet to be, and the final end of history can be made sure and safe' (p. 65). This view is described as 'lying midway between the extremes of optimism and pessimism'! A similar attitude, but from a strictly theistic and Thomist angle, can be seen, e.g., in Garrigou-Lagrange's *La Providence et la Confiance en Dieu* —equally reassuring, pious and hopefully teleological. One could hardly conceive of a better remedy against belief in God! But we must be excused if we prefer real atheists to the meretricious advocates of God's perfections.

with all things. . . . But this I find in all things, that they are more inclined to dance at the feet of Chance. O heaven above me, pure and lofty: that is now to me thought purified—that there is no eternal Reason—Spider and Spider's Net: that thou art a dancing-floor for Divine Chances, a table of the gods for god-like dice and dicers. . . .'

Science may well be built on the fact that in certain directions we find an element of order in the collocation and sequence of phenomena, but in the face of History we are compelled to leap by an act of madness or of faith, or of both, to the conclusion that the realm of History transcends all our scientific concepts and experiences; and though historical events are exposed to influences from the sources known to physiology, biology, geology, and the rest, they are yet always carried by a human being whose uniqueness of character has assimilated the forces of his environment and surpassed them. It is man in his ultimate relationships—his personal initiative and free creativity—who accounts for History.[1]

God and men, then, are the real subjects of History: man in his relation to God and God in his relation to man; and to force historical processes into abstract evolutionary or teleological schemes is to make light of these relations with their, more often than not, lawless, irrational, 'revolutionary' and, generally speaking, eventful character. Man's whole existence is stamped with the unforeseen and unpredictable: his coming and going, his doing and undoing, his fortune and misfortune, indeed, his whole destiny, are incalculables. It is hardly possible to establish any 'continuity of History' until we gain an insight into its points of discontinuity, its contradictions, its leaps and bounds. Who can say why human life should be so full of rapids and whirlpools and hidden sunken rocks or why in the confusion of historical events one element succumbs to destiny, while another becomes destiny itself?[2] And yet all these things

[1] The fallacy of viewing History, and particularly the history of civilizations, as determined by environments, which springs from a failure to conceive the genesis and growth of civilization as acts of creation, is exposed by Toynbee (see op cit. vol i, II C (ii) (b)).

[2] Some interesting evidence of this rationally inexplicable in human History is contained in Antoine Fabre d'Olivet's *Histoire philosophique du genre humain*. For a philosophical discussion of the problem of chance see *Gegenwart* by the Swiss philosopher Eberhard Grisebach.

The insight into the unforeseen, the sudden, the unexpected, the 'chanceful' in human existence was a peculiar gift of the Man of the Renaissance.

are not fortuitous or meaningless: on the contrary, they are
profoundly meaningful; they are the inward logic of a destiny,
of which we may be intensely aware and into which we may
have a prophetic insight, but which is not waiting behind the
scenes to be exhibited when the need arises.

Would it then be true to say that 'man makes History' or, as
the familiar saying goes, 'great men make History'? The question cannot be answered by a simple Yes or No. When the fulness of Time came *God* sent forth his Son. Whenever *God* enters
Time, Time acquires meaning and becomes History: in other
words, the initiative lies with God, and we cannot calculate the
event. Hence issues the distinctly eventful, the new and immeasurable quality of the historical process. It explains the peculiar fact that it is precisely the 'great men' in History who often
realize in their hour of historic decision—whether for or against
God, yet always in conscious or unconscious relation to him—
that they are being led by some mission or calling, that they
are the agents of some supreme agency. Hence also their strange
sensation that they stand, so to say, only behind the events, as if
these occurred against their will, as if they (men) were the ex-
ponents of powers transcending their own faculties. Tolstoy has
shown a great deal of insight when he said that 'in historical
events more clearly than anywhere else the command runs: Do
not eat from the Tree of Knowledge of good and evil. Nothing
but unconscious action bears fruit. An actor in an historical
event never understands its significance. When he tries to see
through it he condemns himself to sterility.' (*War and Peace.*)
But Tolstoy failed to realize the imperative need for man to be
conscious of his historic hour: man cannot but know himself responsible for all that occurs. He is filled with a sense of guilt
when he refuses the call to historical action. History and the
coming of the End are thus also a call to, and an achievement
of, man's creative self-determination. Its character is in this
sense essentially biographical. It may strike us as a strange irony
to proclaim, and apparently to derive comfort from, the fact
that men are the makers of History? Nonetheless it remains true,
even though this making may be degraded into mere 'pornocracy'

'Oh misera Fortuna, quanto sono i tuoi movimenti vari et fallaci nelle
mondane cose!' (Boccaccio.) It hardly needs saying that chance is not the
equivalent of the evil, the untrue and the false as it is with the Idealists or
aitiological theists.

by men who have gathered in themselves the most terrifying mediocrity which betrays their call to creativity and only serves to deepen the void in which our world finds itself.

Nicolas Feodorov, a Russian thinker of amazing boldness and wisdom, inspired by an all-consuming vision of the Christian mystery of God-manhood, spoke of History and the end of this world as depending on a 'human deed', on 'common work', on the directedness of man's whole being towards the universal re-integration of life and the final triumph over death. He was not a 'Pelagian' or a 'humanist' as some believed, however Promethean and phantastic his 'projects' of fighting death appeared to be: rather, he believed that God, who had freed Prometheus from his fetters—chained, as he was, not by God but by the daemons of Nature with whose power he was wrestling—calls man to share in the unceasing divine creative action in the world.[1]

Christ's God-manhood is the call to men to manifest the image of the Maker. Man is creator, though he does not create in his autonomous right, nor as a claim, but rather as a duty before God. And History must be regarded as a divine-human activity presupposing at once divine initiative and human deed. The End is not only to be expected but also to be prepared by man; indeed, expectation itself is fundamentally a creative attitude. The End, as we have seen, is not mere destruction and judgment from without but also man's destiny and vocation, a vocation, that is, to transform the world in the power of his divinely-willed and divinely-given creatorship. 'My Father worketh hitherto and I work' and 'the works that I do shall [he who believes] do also; and greater works than these shall he do.' (John v, 17; xi, 12.) 'Behold, I make all things new'—refers alike to God and men, since God desires the response of man to

---

[1] This is likewise the *leitmotif* of the 'ethics of creativeness' advocated by Nicolas Berdyaev (see, e.g., his *The Destiny of Man*). It is a characteristically Russian conviction, which so often led the Russian people to cast off the burden of fatality. It is particularly true of revolutionary and post-revolutionary Russia. However we interpret the alleged deterministic tendencies of Marxism, there was one vital truth in it whose redeeming influence was as great as many other great ideas that have changed from time to time the current of Russian life. It was the idea, inherited from Christianity, that Fate is an objectification of human impotence and servility, and that man is called upon to share creatively in the making of History. In that thought lies the dynamic that has set Russia free in the Revolution, however much she may still, together with the rest of mankind, be in need of liberation.

the revelation of his Kingdom, which is the 'new heaven' and the 'new earth'. There may be constraint in Evil, and Evil's outcome often appears to have an inexorable, fatal character, but there is nothing inexorable in Good, nor has Good any 'fatal' consequences (despite the venerable fallacy 'virtue its own reward'), because it is a call to freedom, and it is sustained in freedom.

Once more, then, there are no automatically good or compellingly beneficent results in the processes of History, and its End confronts man with a task addressed to his freedom and creativity. Man is called to the re-creating of the natural configuration of all things in and with God. Every truly creative act of man, must, therefore, be regarded as an eschatological act which 'ends' this world and inaugurates a new one. 'If you feed the hungry', writes Berdyaev, 'or free the oppressed, you are committing an eschatological deed, and you are "ending" this world so full of hunger and oppression.' Each truly creative act is a historical fulfilment, a coming of the End, a transcending and transforming of this spellbound, stricken world of ours.

In Manichean dualism, in the deistic world-view of the Enlightenment, in the more recent trends of so-called dialectical theology, as well as in the thought of the modern Existentialists (such as Scheler, Heidegger, Sartre and others)—with, perhaps, the sole exception of Berdyaev and possibly Karl Jaspers —man is divested of his creative destiny, and the world is made devoid of God. That unique event, however, which reveals alike the supreme polarity and unity of God and man, that is, the Incarnation, not only faces man with ultimate decisions, but also imbues him with the *power* to decide, to create, and to act historically. *Finitum capax infiniti: Deus sum ex officio humanitatis meae.* And though the power of man finds its limit in the disintegrating temporality of his creaturely existence, it is nonetheless intensely real, and, in virtue of his relatedness to God, sets free the divine-human potentialities of History.

We shall see later on how these insights (if insights they be) give us the strange awareness of some mysterious guidance or providence which underlies and resolves the multiple events of History, pregnant as they are with contradiction. Such guidance, however, by no means opens up a loophole for new constructions and generalities in the manner of a naïve-realistic belief in providence or otherwise (see the Section on provi-

dence). For providence, which, like everything else, points to
the two-fold mystery of God-manhood, is not a rule of safety:
rather it implies a depth, a risk, a daring, a struggle from which
the abstract generalities of pious theological devices are as
widely removed as possible. But we are brought to a point in
which a unique divine-human event—the Incarnation—has
occurred, thus revealing a new meaning and a new dimension
in History. When we find ourselves in this new dimension every
fragment of Time, every period of History—every man, every
nation, every state, every civilization, every human activity—
are shown to stand in an immediate relation to God: they exist
in their peculiar and unrepeatable situations as an inalienable
part of that great movement of which Christ is the *Alpha* and
Omega, the Beginning and the End. The God-Man reveals himself in the world as it is, not in an imaginary transcendental
world of dreams. In all the events, vicissitudes, turmoils and
perplexities of History Christ's word is being spoken: they are,
in the language of the Fathers, 'dispensations', 'economies',
'testaments'. This cannot be understood as a face-saving method
of acquiescence in the power of His Majesty the Accomplished
Fact in accordance with the motto: 'History is always right.'
Rather, it is an attitude of *understanding*, an apprehension of historical experience, a response to the experienced world which is
adequate to the nature of that experience; but it is very far from
giving one a quiet conscience; it is an awareness of life by which
a meaning is sought in the ambiguous and yet creative forces
of History. . . . Unfortunately, no matter how much people may
profess that the Son of God has descended to earth and is
eternally present on it, it is not this that really concerns them,
but rather that he is now 'in heaven'; no matter how much they
may repeat the prayer that his will be done on earth as it is in
heaven, they nevertheless persist in believing that what is 'in
heaven' is godly, and what is 'on earth' is ungodly. But even the
black stones on the pathways of human destiny are charred
with heavenly fire.

Time, we have found, cannot be estimated from within itself
alone, for its stormy, self-disintegrating flux evades the grasp
of man, who is himself thrown into this movement. But there is,
indeed there must be, a point which is at once within and without Time, from which Time may be known and raised to a historical reality. Such a point could not meet the extreme and

The End

painful situations of temporal existence if it were a mere anonymous spiritual force, an 'ideology', a philosophical idea or human ideal. God himself in the 'existentiality' of his divine-human revelation, that is to say, God in Christ, the Fulness of Time, creates once for all, and thus for ever, the point from out of which Time and all that lives in Time may be known and understood. Knowledge and understanding, therefore, are historic acts of living divine-human relations: a reverting of Time and all things therein to their true depth, to the End.

(b) The New Testament View of History

The preceding considerations may lead us to a much deeper appreciation of the New Testament view of History than many theological textbooks seem to suggest.

We have seen already how much the Christian philosophy of Time differs from the Classical conception of ancient Greece which envisaged the historic process as a kind of treading of the wheel where no new situations are really possible, or a perpetual recurrence as symbolized in the changing rhythms and seasons of the year. Spengler and Nietzsche thought in similar terms. In opposition to this stands the New Testament vision of History which, mathematically speaking, may be described as *victorial* (as distinct from *punctual*), that is to say, its symbol is to be found in a directed magnitude, as of a force or a velocity, or in a directed line which receives its orientation or, since it is a very uneven and broken line, its reorientation from an end. All New Testament utterances in this respect are characterized by such an attitude. 'When the fulness of Time came, God sent forth his Son' (Gal. iv, 4); 'My hour is not yet come' (John ii, 4); 'This is your hour and the power of darkness' (Luke xxii, 53); 'Now is come salvation, and strength, and the Kingdom of our God, and the power of Christ' (Apoc. xii, 10); and the final utterance from the Cross: 'It is finished.' The New Testament, then, testifies to the fact that every point in Time has its own 'situation', not to be repeated or compared with others and moving towards the *telos*, which is within Time and yet beyond it.

There are three New Testament images of History which illustrate this idea: the image of the growing temple (Eph. ii, 19-22: 'Now therefore ye are no more strangers and foreigners, but fellow-citizens with the saints, and of the household of God;

The End

and are built upon the foundation of the apostles and prophets, Jesus Christ himself being the chief corner stone; in whom all the building fitly framed together groweth unto an holy temple in the Lord; in whom ye also are builded together for an habitation of God through the Spirit');[1] further, the image of the tree (see the passages in Rom. xi, referring to the eternal vocation of Israel); and, thirdly, the familiar image of the harvest which, however, is not to be conceived in the Classical way as a cyclic course annually repeating itself, but as a momentous and final event. All these images have one feature in common, viz. that every moment of the proceeding Time has one and only one distinct situation in the historic whole. Every moment bears within itself all the preceding ones and is born of them. The 'first fruits' are born of the 'lump' and 'partake of the root'. The stones above rest on those below and lastly on the 'foundation' and the 'chief corner stone'. In the harvest all the germs and blossoms of the spring and summer attain their fruition. The last stage is thus a *consummation* of the whole process. The godly and the ungodly must confront each other in an all-integrating fulfilment which is a total judgment of History in the light of the final disclosures of its meaning. Then alone can the theme of world-history, the struggle between the divine and the demonic powers, be resolved.

These New Testament ideas laid the foundation not only of the specifically Christian philosophy of History such as that of St. Augustine, Bossuet or Solovyev but of all other philosophies down to that of Marx. Hegel's historico-philosophical conceptions are definitely born of these Christian insights, although the End, the *telos* of the New Testament, had been wholly immanentized by him in the world-process. The more recent Existentialist philosophy is similarly inspired by the essentially Christian conviction that every situation is an 'end', pregnant with a unique and peculiar message and revelation. Each time is in need of its own ethic, because it has its own incomparable ethos, or quality and character. We cannot but endorse these views, even though such endorsement requires certain qualifications.[2] And while, in a sense, every historic moment is the same, in as much as it is what it is only in relation to God, yet, in another sense, each one has its *own* relation to God unlike any other, and

[1] Cf. also the ecclesiological imagery in *Pastor Hermas*.
[2] See below, Part III.

The End

hence exhibits a unique, unrepeatable relation of God to it. It is a distinct point, an event on the line of directed Time—*kairos*, that is, the significant 'highlight', the pregnant moment, the 'particular' in the chain of happenings which achieves a decisive present. '*And that, knowing the time* (εἰδότες τὸν καιρόν), *that now it is high time to awake out of sleep: for now is our salvation nearer than we believe.*' (Rom. xiii, 11.) The present hour, therefore, has, relatively to the previous one, a different 'distance' from the last hour. Everything depends on knowing the hour in which we live and have our being—*eidotes ton kairon. Timeliness* is the great category of Christian life and thought. As a matter of fact, simple common sense prompts us that a thing is right when it comes in due time; and it is wrong when it is belated or premature. Untimely actions are often nothing but barricades against the full reality of life; and unless we are prepared to give up rules and principles when they do not fit life and give preference to life, in other words, unless we are ready to fall back upon more timely convictions, we grow pedantic. Unfortunately people persist in going to moralists for general rules and principles; and since moralists are human they keep themselves busy supplying the market with such rules and principles. For a Christian to be aware of and accept the uniqueness and particularity of his present historic situation is an act of simple obedience to God, since the domain where God is revealed is the domain of Time. True Christian life and thought know no 'always'. There can, therefore, in the last resort, be no 'perennial' philosophy, and it is not indispensable to be obsessed by Time in order to refuse to repeat for our own time what has been said by Aristotle, or Aquinas, or Spinoza, or Kant, however great their historical significance and hence the need of accepting them in their own distinctiveness, of understanding them and of seeing them in true perspective, may be.

There is however more to this than a mere readiness to 'apply' certain permanent and stable principles or norms to indefinitely variable vicissitudes and changing circumstances of Time and History. God cannot in any sense be applied, stuck on or fitted in. It is imperative to discern the creative word of truth for and in the present hour: God cannot be had at less expense. We must fulfil our divine-human destiny and be 'children of our time' in the true and most profound sense of the expression. God's own eternal 'laws' are not an abstract system of rules:

they have their specific historic time like any other phase of divine creation. 'My Father worketh hitherto and I work.' 'This one thing I do, forgetting those things which are behind, and reaching forth unto those things which are before, I press toward the mark for the prize of the high calling of God in Christ Jesus.' (Phil. iii, 13-14.) Jesus Christ is assuredly the same, yesterday, to-day and for ever; yet he is not a ready-made datum, a *Deus ex machina*, but the eternally *new* One. That is why true Christian life and thought involve the membership of a living divine-human body, the Church, which exists not to represent a universal truth but, rather, arising as it does out of an historical event, to live the truth as a revelation in and of History.

Once again we are brought face to face with the Christian mystery of God-manhood with which all life is bounded; for, inasmuch as God reveals himself in and to man, this revelation is an event in Time presupposing a relation of the one who reveals to the one to whom the revelation is made, in other words, it rests on the 'timeful', living mind of God who acknowledges for Himself as well as for His creature the full reality of Time. . . . We shall, however, return to this subject of the 'timefulness' of God at a later stage.

The practical implication of the New Testament view of History from the End is that every turning point in the life of human individuals and of the body politic of men, every social perplexity must be met with the question not primarily as to whether they are good or bad, as to whether they do or do not accord with the 'ideals' of Christianity, but rather as to the light that is thrown on these events from the End; in other words as to whether they represent a manifest destiny, which may be a judgment as well as a promise; whether they are arbitrary and fortuitous or, on the contrary, inwardly motivated. And once they are seen from the End, they represent, as it were, the end of History in fulfilment of its actual end. Our whole life depends, in fact, on whether we know what hour has struck, on whether God's last word has been spoken. This vision underlies the struggles of the Christian Church in History. In particular, it may be regarded as the driving conviction behind the attitude of Eastern Christendom with regard to the problem of Church and the world. The Orthodox Christian could never conceive his place in society as that of a crusader or a reformer (in the sense in which this is true in various degrees of the Western

The End

Christian): rather he knows himself a pilgrim in this stricken and hallowed world of ours, who is resolved to bear its presence patiently in and around himself to the end. And in that very resolution he is given the power to change the world—from within, as part of it in better and in worse, rather than from without, as its censor or its slave. He is thereby fulfilling a prophetic calling, for it is the prophets who introduce us, even before Christ, to the vision of God who redeems the world by experiencing as no other can or does, and by being involved in, the evil and sorrowful pathways of men; and it is the prophets who themselves responded to the challenge of their environment by proclaiming the End through self-identification with the world 'in righteousness, and in judgment, and in loving kindness, and in mercies'. (Hosea.[1])

The eschatological attitude is doubtless subject to certain pitfalls. One might, for instance, be tempted to 'date' the End or to indulge in fanciful interpretations of historical events. But all such attempts, which have frequently made the Christian hope disreputable, cannot undermine the real core of the truth: the truth, that is, that the End is coming and is already here, and that from this End Time acquires meaning and History is being fulfilled. The Christian lives not *at* the End of Time, but rather *from* the End and *in* the End of Time.

The New Testament finds the beginning of the new world and the pledge of the final end of Time in Christ's return in glory and in judgment. Now the expectation of the second coming of Christ is not a phantastic dream but a sober and inevitable conviction of our faith, which discloses the truth about Time. We cannot avoid recognizing that the record of Christ, the Lord of Glory, being rent asunder and destroyed by men is the affirmation of an apparently irreconcilable contradiction, which, nevertheless, unless God is no God, presses for a solution. Man may have got used to the Gospel story of God's mortal agony and death (though can anybody 'get used' to it if he really *heard* it once?) but he has hardly been able to contain or comprehend its terrifying mysteriousness. The sheer fact that the one who commands the heavens and the earth must ask, beseech, invite men to

[1] It is significant that the Old Testament prophets describe their relation with Israel on the analogy of the intimate communion which characterizes the experience of sexual love. Hosea receives the command of God to marry a harlot (namely Israel).

receive him: this alone appears to contradict all that God is and
signifies. How are we to understand this singularly paradoxical
situation? It is not made meaningful by mere references to the
enmity of the Jews or the godlessness of the Gentiles. The
raison d'être must lie elsewhere: it lies above all with the fact of
human freedom (see below); and it lies also with the mystery
of God's revelation in Time. The *kenosis* or self-limitation of God
arises with His coming into Time and, indeed, with the very
emergence of Time. What is present in Time cannot be omni-
present. It must needs arise at and issue from a definite point
and thence extend in concentric waves. God must humiliate
Himself to show His mercy towards men, plunged as they are
into the deadly stream of temporality: 'And being found in
fashion as a man, he humbled himself and became obedient
unto death, even the death of the cross.' God does not become,
even in Christ, visible in the strict sense of the word; He does
not impose Himself on men: He remains hidden in His very
presence. And yet God does show His glory in Christ and reconcile the world unto Himself, and the results of the world's
alienation from Him must and can be finally overcome. The
cloud which conceals Christ's presence must vanish and He
must become visible as He is. 'Now are we the sons of God, and
it does not yet appear what we shall be: but we know that when
he shall appear, we shall be like him; for we shall see him as
he is.' (1 John iii, 2; cf. Apoc. i, 7.) A supreme and open con-
frontation between God and man must take the place of God's
hidden presence. There will be 'judgment'—not, surely, in the
sense of a trial at which men are to be acquitted or condemned
in the sight of a revengeful Godhead in respect of all the good or
wrong that they have committed (a conception which has played
a considerable part in certain types of Christian theology and
popular belief), but in the sense of a 'crisis', a disclosure, divul-
gence of the true situation, a disclosure which is concomitant with
the very fact that Christ is to be a visible reality in the co-inherence of his divine-human being. In this sense not only man but
God waits on the Last Judgment: 'O Jerusalem, Jerusalem, which
killeth the prophets and stoneth them that are sent unto thee;
how often would I have gathered thy children together, as a hen
doth gather her brood under her wings, and ye would not! Behold,
your house is left unto you desolate: and verily I say unto you, Ye
shall not see me, until the time come when ye shall say, Blessed

The End

is he that cometh in the name of the Lord.' (Luke xiii, 34-5.)

This ultimate disclosure of God, however, is also a redemption, a sanctification and a *theosis* or deification, not a mere manifestation. It is something that God not only shows but does in the power of His God-manhood. Hence issues the vision of a 'new heaven' and a 'new earth', a new creation, as it is recorded in the Apocalypse. It signifies the appearance of a new corporeity and the resurrection of the dead. The Christian affirmation of and belief in the resurrection must inevitably conflict with Hellenic and, particularly, Platonic dualism. Platonism and Christianity alike think in terms of two realms of being. But Platonism (and its Christian and non-Christian adepts) conceive of two worlds which are related to each other as two layers superimposed one upon the other. Such 'static' dualism spells resignation in regard to temporal and historical reality. Christianity, on the other hand, conceives of this relation as one at once of co-inherence (or one might say in-ordination), and of tension which presses towards a solution. Such 'dynamic' dualism is really a struggle for *visibility*. Our present order is a reign of the temporal which conceals the visibility of God. 'Blessed are they that have not seen, and yet have believed.' But the emergence of the new order is to be a visible disclosure of God's Kingdom, which until then is kenotically hidden within the ambiguities of Time. The final consummation, then, is a visible disclosure of the Kingdom, a rending of the veil in order to make manifest a hitherto invisible presence.

This presupposes yet another mysterious fact, to which St. Paul and St. John testify, namely, that Christ in His resurrection has actually entered the 'new heaven' and the 'new earth' as the 'first fruits' and the initiator of a new world-order. Indeed, everyone partakes, in the power of the risen Lord, already here and now of the transfigured cosmos. We are not observers of Christ's resurrection, but share in it and are actuated by it. We must affirm, therefore, that in this relation to Christ's resurrection everyone has already received the new corporeity (an implication which is experienced with particular intensity in the Eastern Orthodox tradition),[1] though this fact is still inaccessible to empirical perception. This is not to be confused with

[1] Hence the extremely realistic and almost physical Orthodox conception of salvation and sanctification. We do not blush because of this. On the contrary, we believe it to aim at the very heart of the Christian hope.

the speculations of occultism or anthroposophy, since the new corporeity is not something that can be fixed or objectified within a world of extraneous things and objects: 'Ye are dead, and your life is hid with Christ in God.'

The final disclosure of the already operative new corporeity is the resurrection of the dead. The certainty that we have already passed from death to life is not opposed to the other fact that 'we shall rise again on the last day': rather, the one presupposes the other. For whenever we become aware of the new being in Christ as actually present, we also realize the tension which urges towards ultimate fulfilment, and we struggle for the visibility of that which is given us invisibly. Hence the close connection between the two affirmations in Johannine writings: 'He who believes in me has already risen from death to life' (John v, 24), and 'I will raise him up at the last day' (John vi, 39). But the connection is evident only on the condition that we eliminate radically from biblical theology the abstract notions of a rationalistic and atomistic philosophy.

The disclosure of the new world cannot, however, be confined to man as part of the creation, since he is not a 'part' of it but a microcosmos. The 'new heaven' and the 'new earth' are not the result of a kind of reconstruction which proceeds by way of the reconditioning of certain sections (the top or the wing) of a building, but a reintegration of the whole. 'For we know that the whole creation groaneth and travaileth in pain together until now', and, 'expects the manifestation of the sons of God.' (Rom. viii, 22, 19.) The apocalyptic image of birthpains, descriptive of the bringing forth of the new world, shows a real identity between life upon this earth and the age to come, though this identity can be properly realized and understood only through having realized and understood the transcendence and otherness of the latter. In other words, what happens here on earth is transcended through being taken up into 'Life eternal', so that the character of the present temporal existence and the character of earthly and bodily life are of eternal significance. Indeed, there is not the smallest hair of our head that will be discarded: *this* corruptible must put on incorruption as surely as it is corruptible, as surely as it must die. Such is the paradox of the Christian Easter message, and we shall have to remember it in all our subsequent discussion of the relation between God and the world.

Part II

THE BEGINNING AND THE END

Chapter I

THEODICY

It is not easy to discuss in the now prevailing theological and philosophical atmosphere the old dilemma of theodicy or, to give this term its accepted definition, of the vindication of divine providence and government in view of the existence of evil in the world. We have come to realize that it is pointless and indeed preposterous to make God into a 'problem' or an 'object of discussion'. Most theodicies, even the most venerable ones, refer not to God but to a dubious figment of the human brain, in need of justification, apologetics and proofs of its reality. This 'God' is no God but an idol: men create such gods in their own image, and the gods grow old along with the men that made them. We may, together with the atheists, legitimately defy him and his claims. The problem of these theodicies is in every sense an unreal, irrelevant problem. It is impossible to pass judgment on God, since He is 'beyond good and evil', in the true and absolute meaning of this expression: He is, that is to say, the source of all our judgments. The only conceivable theodicy, it would seem therefore, is one which establishes the difference between the reality of God and the human, all-too-human idea of Him, rather than one which attempts to defend God against Himself.

And yet, what are we to say of the stern and pain-ridden destiny of man, in the face of which all our attempts at consolation are like dust and ashes in his mouth? We cannot explain away or whittle down this human condition. The desperate question which drove the mind of Dostoevsky's Ivan Karamazov and many others mad makes the God of other worldly rewards and retributions no God. How are we to relate the fact of human tragedy which pervades man's whole existence to God's eternal justice? After all, asking thus, *knocking*, is not the same as posing irrelevant or preposterous questions. 'Knocking' is not easy, and few are capable of doing it. That is, perhaps, why it is not opened to us. Men prefer to produce ingenious systems and con-

structions instead of listening and seeking: that is to say, be-
having in a way which alone brings forth questions worth the
answering.

'O, that thou wouldst rend the heavens, that thou wouldst
come down on the oppressed and stricken by victorious evil and
iniquity, by meaninglessness, suffering and desperation! . . .'
This is not a speculative 'question' which can be objectified and
made into a matter of intellectual reflections, or dealt with by
ready-made answers or by dismissal. It speaks of man's tragic
awareness of his ultimate relation to God, and unless we are
ready to run the risk of being partners in this human situation,
we shall not understand man at all. Can we look into the world
from the allegedly safe and undisturbed domain of 'religion'
without being caught by the longing and afflictions of this
world? It is the understanding of these profoundly human issues,
pressing forward and winning meaning, which justifies the problem of theodicy. It will, moreover, easily be seen that, as such,
these issues must be considered in the context of the discussion
of the meaning of History. But it is nobody's business to offer
'solutions': there are none, and he who thinks he can produce
them shows that he has not even begun to think about real
problems. However much philosophers and theologians may
claim to penetrate into the mysteries of God and man and
assume the posture of omniscient oracles when confronted with
such issues, they thereby betray, in fact, their helpless ignorance
and pitiable perplexity.

(a) Man in Revolt

It is a fallacy to believe that man naturally seeks his own
happiness and perfection. On the contrary, pain and pleasure,
joy and sorrow, hopes, fears, passions, expectations, devotion,
anger, love and hate, in short, all that fills the human mind and
heart and of which human speech can tell only in approximation—all these things are hardly meant for the happiness or
comfort of the human individual, much less of the human species
as a whole. Man is an exceedingly irrational being: he easily and
deliberately defies the most unmistakably reasonable course of
action and trots jauntily into a jungle of irreconcilable contradictions, without considering in the least his own felicity.

In his *Memoirs from the Underground* Dostoevsky shows man as

being prone to upset the whole rational order and the most desirable harmony of life for the sole reason of asserting his own will. It is indeed not infrequent that man rejects his own happiness, such a transitory moment as it is in the torrent of general destruction. He defies and sets himself against the very fact of his existence; he refuses to accept it as his own and rises against the ground from whence he came, even if it may involve him in self-annihilation. Dostoevsky shows that, as a matter of fact, this attitude is a pledge of real freedom. Man's freedom involves an unlimited capacity of self-assertion: yea, a readiness to challenge God, even while ultimately aware of the immeasurable pain of his own impotence; man does not yield to any power, even that of God, until *God* yields, accedes, 'repents'. If he resigns from the struggle, it is only a truce in which, beneath the mask of reconciliation, the old enmity persists, and an awful revenge is in preparation.[1] The dignity of man spells a two-fold capacity for revolt and humility in the face of God: defiance and self-abandonment in love are the indelible signs of his true God-given manhood. His godlessness and godliness are alike the supreme condition of the divine image in him. *Nemo contra Deum sine Deus ipse.* The real significance of consistent revolt lies, therefore, in that it confronts man with God. The posture of rising against God is, metaphorically speaking, the same as raising a clenched fist which may not be opened and is yet unable to strike: for were it to strike as if to reach God, it would exhaust itself in nothingness. The disquiet and the terror of persistent defiance threaten its very persistency, and in that tension there dwells a readiness to love and to surrender oneself. Herein lies the truth of Luther's enigmatic dictum that blasphemy sometimes sounds more agreeable in God's ears than Halleluiah or a solemn hymn of praise, 'and the more frightful and repulsive the blasphemy, the more agreeable it is to God' (quanto enim horribilior et foedior est blasphemia, tanto est Deo gratior). There is but one step, if as much as one, between the infamous and the 'famous', and the final and most radical challenge calls forth the first real answer. In the last mortal terror we hear the words:

[1] This may appear to be a very spectacular and high-pitched form of atheism. The atheism of the 'average European' is rather different. If, as Carlyle remarked, Christ were to come to-day people would not even crucify Him: they would ask Him to dinner and hear what He had to say, and probably enjoy themselves. But these idiosyncrasies do not invalidate the problem before us.

peace be unto you! Indeed, 'there are questions which it would be impossible to ask if they did not contain an intrinsic answer, questions we could not even approach without the courage of Augustine: Thou wouldst not seek me hadst thou not already found me.' (Karl Barth.) Man's godlessness is a witness to God: 'Surely the wrath of man shall praise Thee.' (Ps. lxxvi, 10). . . .

But the peace thus gained bears within itself the experience which comes through transcended revolt, and the new happiness of self-surrender in God is a fruit of experienced freedom and self-determination in a life lived out to its end and beyond itself. Indeed, no one is entitled to deny or, for that matter, to regret or slight or praise, the experiences of his freedom, for to do so amounts to desecrating one's own destiny. Doubtless a sinner can and must repent: it is the only thing he can do. But even the most zealous penitential drummers would grant that repentance is no denial of one's past: on the contrary, it is a moment of initiation by which the past acquires new meaning. The Greeks believed that even the gods cannot change the past. But Christ not only changed the past but re-wrote it; and sinful man can do likewise, for only a soul scorched by deprivation and depth of sin can ask for God's redeeming mercy. The moment the prodigal son fell on his knees and wept, he made his past sacred moments in his life.

(b) Some Interpretations of Human Destiny

Man who has experienced the rebirth into a new life and vision, pregnant as they are with the awareness of previous torment, is pressed forward to motivate and to sustain his experience on intellectual grounds, and this results in the various attempts to conceive a theodicy: How could God in the almightiness and goodness of his nature create this universe and allow its evil and injustice? How are we to understand and to explain all that which denies Meaning and Value in this world of ours? The more we despair of the solutions in a mere otherworldly transcendentalism, the more intense becomes the need for some adjustment.

In the Indian solution of the great riddle of the origin of suffering and the diversity of human conditions we find an impersonal universal law with its attendant *karma*. In a metempsychosis, which elevates or reduces the human soul to all the

Theodicy

forms in the hierarchy of the animated world, man's previous existence, good and evil, is being rewarded or expiated by way of various rebirths. All existence is thus governed by a rigid system of moral requital, although one is not necessarily imbued with any memories of previous existence. Everyone makes his or her own present lot and is to make the succeeding ones. The meaning of a moral action is aimed at a better reincarnation and ultimately at a liberation from all metempsychoses. This doctrine claims to solve all the problems of evil rationally, without even raising in any serious way the question of theodicy: in its stead it puts the concept of an inexorable immanental law which governs all existence. However, quite apart from its inherent anthropological difficulties, notably its exclusion of any genealogy representing a procession of unique, distinct and abiding human beings, this doctrine, though it points, admittedly, to the problem in question, does not meet the predicament of man: it reduces his destiny in a rather mechanical way to mere 'past acts' or 'psychological states' and their living down in an infinite future.[1]

Zoroastrianism, especially in its later developments, as also Manichean and Gnostic thinkers, taught a dualism in which God was divested of his absoluteness and set against an independent evil power (or a demiurge): there are from the beginning two principles, and evil and imperfection are the result of a partial victory of the evil power which overshadows the light of the Divine. The world is a battlefield between a good and an evil God, or it is the very product of the latter, and his action in producing it is a retaliation against the Lord of Light. And though the ultimate victory of the latter seems to be assured, nonetheless meanwhile the whole world-process epitomizes the unrelieved and unrelievable pain of meaninglessness. The rays of Light scattered here and there within this world must be freed from the surrounding and prevailing darkness and return through a final separation of good and evil to the source of Light.[2] Such a dualism is in some sense more impressive than Indian monism. It makes, however, nonsense of the very idea of God, and gives the lie to our real concern: namely, to find a meaning in the here and now of human existence.

There is yet another doctrine which must be considered in

[1] See Charles Eliot, *Hinduism and Buddhism.*
[2] See Sydney Cave's *Introduction to Study of Living Religions of the East.*

the discussion of the relation of human destiny to God, which pertains to the specifically Christian world of ideas and experiences, viz. the doctrine of predestination.

The principal assertion of predestinarianism is that God remains essentially beyond the sphere of any human claims. God's counsels are as inscrutable as they are fixed. They determine every man's destiny in Time and in Eternity. Man's being and doing on earth does not, therefore, mean that he can modify or change God's counsels concerning him or his own destiny: rather, we are to perceive in them mere signs of his election or reprobation, as the case may be.

The consistent articulation of this doctrine belongs to St. Augustine. Theological Augustinianism is indeed often primarily associated with the doctrine of unconditional predestination. But over and above this it involves a characteristic doctrine of man, which in its turn determined the philosophy of freedom for centuries to come. Augustine did not always teach predestinarianism in its radical form, though he did so in the last twenty years of his life, and has demanded that this should be regarded as his final view. The doctrine was provoked by, and attained its complete definition in the struggle with, Pelagian moralism, but actually it was already implicit in Augustine's initial philosophical outlook. He maintained from the outset that man is free only in the sense of *being freed* or liberated (*liberatio*) by God; and, while in a sense he allowed of a *conversio ad Deum*, he was, nevertheless, consistent enough to regard humanity as a *massa iustae damnationis*, incapable of responding to God, so that the free agency of man does not really enter into the divine plan of salvation. Indeed, no one would have had any right to complain or to impugn God's justice if the dread sentence of reprobation had been carried out in full, and the whole of humanity consigned to damnation for ever. But since God is *omnipotentissimus* he can elect and call in Time certain favoured individuals out of the 'damned mass' as vessels of his mercy, who cannot resist his grace; the rest are subject to a decree of reprobation or at least of *preterition* or 'passing over', and 'they steadily gravitate, under the inexorable pressure of the divine justice, towards the bottomless pit'.[1] The *numerus clausus* (that is to say, the declaration of Augustine that the 'lists' of the elect and reprobate are closed) signifies, in fact,

---

[1] N. P. Williams, *The Ideas of the Fall and of Original Sin*, p. 376.

68

the annulment of freedom. The Pauline 'foreknowledge' in the sense of a divine-human synergism with its implicit recognition of man's freedom is thereby completely destroyed, and we are faced with a system of unmitigated divine determinism.[1] *Deus facit, ut velimus bonum, Deus agit motum voluntatis, inclinat voluntatem, praeparat voluntatem.* This view was strengthened by Augustine's physical interpretation of original sin, with its pre-established pneumato-somatic dualism, its radical contempt of physical passion, and its erroneous belief that the process of human generation is in itself sinful, or that sin is conveyed to the offspring because of the sinfulness of that process: *concupiscentia radix omnium peccatorum!* . . . It is strange that the disastrous aberrations of predestinarianism should have been initiated by a Christian teacher who had grounded his whole philosophy in the idea of love.[2]

[1] All New Testament scholars seem to agree that the deterministic conclusions of predestinarianism are in no way warranted by St. Paul's thought, whose general practice is to state alternately two apparently contradictory propositions (in this case divine sovereignty and human freedom) without attempting to harmonize these by means of deductive logic. . . . It should be noted that the theology of the Reformation and particularly Calvinism, with its consistent voluntaristic predestinarianism (reaffirmed in the modern radical Calvinism of Karl Barth), has, it would seem, failed to express St. Paul's and, generally speaking, the New Testament's profoundly antinomic position with regard to the question of grace and freedom which he and the later Christian Fathers view in Christological terms, in terms of the indissoluble mystery of divine-human co-inherence. 'Work out your own salvation with fear and trembling; for it is God which worketh in you both to will and to do. . . .' (Phil. ii, 12-13.) 'Behold, I stand at the door and knock: if any man hear my voice and open the door, I will come into him, and will sup with him and he with me.' (Apoc. iii, 20.) The Eastern Fathers, though quite erroneously accused of semi-Pelagianism—whatever this may mean—have in fact throughout maintained the double emphasis of the biblical view. In doing so they were compelled to repudiate the notion of 'prevenient grace' inasmuch as it spells a dichotomy of the mystery of God-manhood and implies that God only wills to bestow this grace upon a given number of men, and consequently must be deemed to will the non-salvation of those on whom he does not bestow it.

[2] An even more radical and crudely fatalistic predestinarianism is expressed in Islamic theology, particularly in the doctrine of *kismet*. Although this doctrine seems to have been originally designed as a compromise between extreme fatalism and extreme libertarianism, man's task is here seen as confined to the acceptance of a fate already allotted to him by God, and he is thereby reduced to an automaton, though 'part of his machinery is that he believes himself free'.

It is a well-known fact that, paradoxically, predestinarianism had in no way weakened the will of those who held this belief but, on the contrary, stimulated them to very energetic action. This is true not only of the Mohammedans but also of the various types of Calvinists. They acted on the

The Beginning and the End

St. Thomas Aquinas's position in this respect does not appear to differ much from the Augustinian doctrine, although he was probably less consistent than the great African Father.

Predestination, according to Aquinas, is the providence of God in relation to 'rational creatures'; he alone can give them the 'ultimate end', i.e. can 'appoint their order' (*Summa theol.* i, qu. 9). In virtue of this decree God determines the 'number of the elect', and in so far as it belongs to divine providence to permit some to turn away from eternal life, so also it belongs to it that God should reprobate some. 'Therefore, as predestination includes the will to confer grace and glory; so also reprobation includes the will to permit a person to fall into sin, and to impose the punishment of damnation on account of that sin.' St. Thomas asserts with not very comforting sternness that reprobation is also a good: 'God loves all men and all creatures, inasmuch as he wishes them all some good; but He does not wish every good to them all (*non tamen quod cunque bonum vult omnibus*). So far, therefore, as He does not wish this particular good, namely eternal life, He is said to hate or reprobate them.' According to this, then, there is also a good which is a good for God but not for His creatures. Indeed, hell, to put it rather crudely, is a source of comfort to God, inasmuch as it vindicates His justice.

It was not easy for St. Thomas to construe the doctrine of freedom on these premises, even though he maintains that 'reprobation by God does not take anything away from the power of the person reprobated' and that 'when it is said that the reprobated cannot obtain grace, this must not be understood as implying absolute impossibility but only conditional impossibility'. It was not easy to vindicate freedom, because in the doctrine of God he had applied throughout the idea of the sole divine 'causality'; and in the doctrine of the *gubernatio* (S. th. i, 103) had shown that the *finis mundi*, just as the *principium mundi*, is *aliquid extra mundum*. But if the world has no self-existent being, it follows that the *gubernatio* must be conceived as implying that by God alone all things are determined in their being, their

assumption that the world is already disposed for the best by the will of a transcendent power of which some men must necessarily be the chosen instruments against whom, therefore, 'the gates of hell cannot prevail' (see R. H. Tawney, *Religion and the Rise of Capitalism*). The manifest and not uncommon pitfall in this conviction is that those who are thus convinced assume that their own will is identical with the will of God!

Theodicy

becoming and their final attainment; for they themselves 'cannot move forward to that which is extrinsic [*sic!*] to the whole universe.' Aquinas, however, claims to safeguard free will, which, indeed, he even postulates, but, significantly enough, in view of its 'meritorious' character (ibid. I, 83).[1] In accordance with this it is even emphasized that the process of grace is realized with the consent of free will, which consent, however, is at the same time the 'effect' of grace (see below). The same thing is said of the virtues.

We must conclude that the doctrine of predestination is a refusal to face the problem of theodicy, since it divests man of his freedom by denying the *reciprocal* character of his relation to God, although, characteristically enough, it has resulted in a highly rationalized theological structure, with all the paraphernalia of subtle scholastic distinctions, which claims to meet all the difficulties involved in that problem.

Having thus convinced ourselves of the breakdown of predestinarianism, or for that matter of any rounded off system of solving the mystery of man's destiny and its relation to God, we are left with the only possible way, namely, that of trying to understand the significance of this very mysteriousness. Our searching mind does not acknowledge any limits in asking and seeking, though it does recognize limits and limitations in supplying answers. The real issue is that of understanding the place and function of man's freedom in its faculty of defiance and self-abandonment, on the one hand, and this freedom's relation to the freedom of God, on the other. The precariousness and vulnerability of all rational theodicies is really an appeal to the exercise of our freedom; and it is the formidable problem of freedom, or rather one aspect of that problem, that we shall now endeavour to discuss.

(c) *Freedom*

There is something utterly elusive about freedom—the fact of freedom rather than the concept thereof. Not unlike Time freedom cannot be defined. We can become aware of the reality of freedom or we may be able to describe it phenomenologically,

---

[1] To deny freedom is wrong, he says elsewhere, because this opinion 'takes away the rewards and punishments of the future life' (tollit enim praemis et. poenas futurae vitae) (*Questiones disputatae cum quodlib.*, qu. de spirit. creat. ix).

but we can form no adequate concept of freedom: all such conceptualizations or rationalizations, as Bergson has reminded us, usually result in the disappearance of freedom and sooner or later pay the penalty of deep and tormenting disappointment. It is impossible to speak of freedom in a language that is purged of contradictions if one wishes one's words to correspond even approximately to reality. The nearest and simplest we can say —and this is probably the most conclusive 'definition' of freedom—it that it is a state of inward self-determination as opposed to every kind of determination from without, that is to say, to every kind of compulsion: it is a reality belonging to the realm of inwardness as opposed to that of outwardness. To take a few examples at random: the Eastern Fathers defined freedom as *autarky* (αὐτάρκεια in Antiochean theology), meaning that the free man is 'self-sufficient'), governs his own life without constraint from any external cause.[1] Thomas Aquinas spoke of the will which moves itself (novet se ipsum, *S. th.* ix, 3);[2] and Hegel understood freedom as 'to be in possession of oneself', or as the spirit who is 'conscious of himself as his own world and conscious

---

[1] A later Eastern Father, Gregory Palamas, little known in the West but immensely important, describes freedom as *aut'exousia*, a term usually denoting God's omnipotence. This point is made clear in a discussion of the nature of the angels who, though hierarchically superior to men, are yet shown to be inferior to them in the general scheme of divine economy. 'There is nothing higher than man' (οὐδὲν ἀνθρώπου κρεῖττον, Migne, P. G. cl, c. 1145-48 and c. 1165). The reason for this is man's 'faculty to exercise dominion'; for, Palamas explains, there is in the nature of our soul something dominant and absolute (ἀρχικόν), and through our capacity to reign God possesses power over the world (ibid.). The other feature which reveals the pre-eminence of men over angels is their 'creativity from nothing' (προάγειν ἐκ μὴ ὄντων), though not from complete non-being (μή ἐκ μηδαμῶς ὄντων, ibid.). This latter point is then shown to be the source and supreme justification of man's creative achievements in science, art, handicraft, and so forth.

[2] This idea, however, is weakened by St. Thomas's general tendency to divine determinism, for the will is not a creative principle but a 'secondary' cause (see below), *potentia qua volumus*, or *naturalis motus*, something, that is to say, which is, aitiologically and teleologically speaking, entirely determined from without (quod est extrinsecum). The will is dependent on willing an extraneous object, and hence on the intellect which, so to say, moves it (the will) through the presentation of an object to be willed. For St. Bonaventure, on the contrary, and, as we believe, much more convincingly, free will is a *totum potentiale*—the operative unity of spirit and will ('consensus rationis et voluntatis' or 'facultas potentiarum', *Commentaria in iv L.* sent. ii. d.); his conclusion, therefore, that freedom operates 'ex sui ipsius imperio et dominio' strikes us as much more consistent. See E. Gilson, *La philosophie de St. Bonaventure*.

of the world as himself'. (*Phaenomenologie des Geistes*, vi.)[1]

All these descriptions express the nature of man as he is ultimately aware of himself. If man reflects on what he means by calling himself *I*, he discerns that he is thereby making an act of freedom, of creative self-determination. *I* is essentially self-originating, issuing from itself, from within outward. It is a subject that makes *itself* an object—not, however, in the sense in which the things of this divided world present themselves to it as something external to it, but in a unique way by which its (the subject's) objective givenness inheres in its very subjectivity. 'I am' signifies 'I posit myself' or 'I create myself'. This self-creative character of everyone capable of saying *I* can be illustrated with reference to grammar. *I* is a pronoun, a grammatical form which expresses the originality and uniqueness of man uttering 'I'. *The* (or an) *I*, on the contrary, is a completely artificial and meaningless substantive which denotes the objectiveness of the self but is, in fact, an unreality, for *I* is never an object. Such a manner of speech is the result of an evil inevitability of making an object of everything we are talking about, even when this is actually impossible. By uttering 'I am' I establish my own existence: I do not say 'something about myself' as a heterogeneous individual entity to be approached by me from without; rather, my very utterance is an act of inward self-initiation. Even doubts of one's existence or the desire for one's own annihilation is dissolved in the very fact of such doubting or desiring: it is an act of freedom and self-assertion.[2]

Such then is the nature of freedom: it is creative and self-determinative, i.e. an activity of self-origination, of being and becoming oneself. This accounts for the profoundly irrational nature of freedom: it is the embodiment of self-sufficiency and independence. Subjicite et dominami! And, maybe, unless freedom is annihilated there can be no order: there will always be chaos rather than Euclidian harmony and law.

It would, however, be quite wrong to conclude from this that freedom is a nisus of self-assertion, a bare identity, a kind of unrelated, lifeless, tautologous judgment: I—I; or that freedom

---

[1] Kant and Fichte went so far as to substitute the 'infinite moral will' for the transcendent God of Christian theism—a dehumanizing tendency characteristic of all Idealism.

[2] Dostoevsky has shown with amazing insight and power how extreme nihilism is in the end one with extreme self-affirmation (cf. Kirilov in *The Possessed*).

necessitates an attitude of egotism and solipsism which acknowledges the sole reality of one's own self. There are few philosophers who have stood for solipsism (Max Stirner is probably the only consistent one among them[1]), although there are plenty of people who are solipsists in their life and their behaviour. Man is rather prone to make himself the centre of the universe and to look at everything from out of the sombre pit of his self-centredness. This state of mind results in frittering away existence in pursuit of one's own shadow, in a loss of perspective, in the inability to see and discriminate between the realities of life: it is the failure *to transcend* oneself. Le moi est haïssable (Pascal). As a matter of fact self-transcendence is the hall-mark of true freedom; and the depth of my freedom is measured by my capacity to transcend and to outgrow myself. Freedom is 'eccentric'; it is an act of existentiality, that is to say, in the language of Existentialism, a 'standing out' (*ex-sistere*), an emergence, a transcending. Self-transcendence, however, involves not only a surpassing of certain parts or aspects of the order of my own divided nature, not a mere 'widening of outlook', but a coming into relation with realities which are not themselves given as part of that order, with a Reality that is other than and beyond myself, though, evidently, this 'beyond' cannot be objectified into something external to me. We live in the tension of this twofold awareness of our selfs as issuing wholly from within ourselves and yet receiving power from beyond our selfs.[2] Our very existence, ambiguous, impotent, and stricken as it is, calls for an answer beyond our comprehension: it may not speak of God, and yet proclaims him in its silence. The very possibility of the free creature questioning about its own existence points to something deeper, to the transcendent, to the other one, to God. In so questioning the creature proves its 'limit', its non-self-sufficiency, and thus reads the transcendent cipher of being enshrined in its inmost structure. In wonder and in shame, in terror and in love, I am brought in my freedom face to face with the living reality of the transcendent.[3]

---

[1] See his *Der Einzige und sein Eigentum*. The demonism of self-centredness is expressed in the unforgettable images of Dante's crepuscular angels who have 'remained by themselves'.

[2] This has been discussed with great insight by Reinhold Niebuhr in his important work *The Nature and Destiny of Man* (see particularly vol. ii, ch. 4).

[3] Nicolas Hartmann, who has given a masterly analysis of the concept of freedom, completely ignores the problem of the ground of man's free

Theodicy

Man, then, creates himself in freedom: yet not from emptiness but in awareness of the transcendent ground of his existence. He is conscious of his freedom and he is thrust upon himself: but in this freedom he is related to transcendent Reality whose will it is that he should confront it in independence, since otherwise he could not be a self. He is responsible for what he wills and what he is 'from the beginning'. He answers for his empirical existence, he makes his choice and bears his guilt, for freedom demands that all he is within and without should be subject to his freedom and responsibility.

The assertion, however, that the true self is no longer the little, narrow self of egotism, but must perennially transcend itself and realize itself in and from the beyond, does not suffice to describe the full content and potentiality of freedom, for these relate not only to the transcendent ground of man's existence but also to the world in which he exists. I live in Time and Space. I live within the cosmic rhythm of Nature which is not an *idolum non loquens,* or a mere material to be used to my advantage (as modern scientific and technical civilization seems to teach us), but the realm of my existence, a reality to be understood and reverenced. 'Do the stars whisper to me? Or do they move dully, like empty pots, according to Copernicus?' (Rozanov) . . . I am endowed with soul and body in which I am active or inert, in which I can experience and endure my strength or weakness, my joy or sorrow. True, there can be no freedom if man is determined from without, whether this 'without' pertains to the realm of nature, of matter or of society. But neither can freedom be regarded as opposed to nature, to matter, or to society, for in these man is united to the created universe and to mankind. Such opposition, characteristic of all kinds of abstract spiritualism, is quite incapable of expressing the fulness and integrality of human existence. In point of fact, true freedom embraces all these realities and signifies their

creative activity—as it were this activity's relational character, and hence arrives at atheism as the necessary condition of moral life. But that is what renders the Hartmannian 'value of human freedom' impotent and meaningless: it remains unrelated to any living reality except that of an abstract realm of 'ideal values', and man appears like a Muenchhausen pulling himself by the hair out of the swamp with the strength of his own arm. 'It is difficult', writes Berdyaev in his forceful critique of Hartmann's position, 'to reconcile the idea of human freedom with the idea of God's existence, and it is equally difficult to recognize freedom if God does not exist.' *The Destiny of Man,* p. 45).

integration in and through man's self-transcendence. The body belongs as much to the reality of the free human being as the spirit and can in no way be abstracted from the 'spiritual' in man. The old-fashioned Cartesian dualism of 'soul' and 'body', of 'spirit' and 'matter' is a real retrogression if compared, for instance, with the more comprehensive Thomist anthropology. There exists but one form of dualism, and a relative dualism at that; the dualism of the 'inward' and the 'outward', of 'History' and 'nature', of 'person' and 'thing', which dualism however has a wholly different connotation.[1] Indeed, man in his bodily existence can free himself from the shackles of outwardness and thinghood and enter into that of spirit and inwardness. This is a fundamental implication of the Christian doctrine of the resurrection of the dead, who are to rise again in body and not merely in spirit. But the risen body is not subject to external determinations, nor is it itself a 'thing' external to other 'things', but a new, spiritual body which is yet opposed to a discarnate, abstract spirit. The doctrine of resurrection is distinguished from that of survival after death, or the immortality of the soul, precisely in that it assumes the reality of eternal life for integral man rather than for a ghostly part of him. And this accounts for the supremely 'humanistic' character of this doctrine.

But man's self-transcendence applies likewise to society. Just as everybody *is* only in as much as he is a body, he cannot be alone but stands in a relation to society, even though he may oppose it. Indeed, our social relations may be so powerful as to change us completely according to the transformations of the social environment and of those to whom we are socially related. And, in particularly primitive spiritual conditions, people, when overwhelmed by the pressure of society, appear completely to lose their self-awareness. The affirmation of man's independence of the power of society, however, in no way involves a dualism between 'person' and 'society', which dualism is a by-product of disintegrated living and thinking. It is this dualism which is responsible for the social order based on independent, atomized units which came into being in the West after the Middle Ages and persisted more or less intact until the first World War, and

[1] 'Nature' in this context does not, of course, signify the cosmos which can in no way be set over against History: what is meant here is a world pervaded by extraneousness—a world of outwardness in which, as Hegel says, 'all things are outside each other'.

Theodicy

whose breakdown we are witnessing to-day. One of its effects was, no doubt, to liberate or to release individual energies and to test the potentialities of human freedom. But this liberation, in its turn, resulted in an unheard of bondage—a bondage to 'things', goods and commodities, money, and other fictitious values vowed to the service of greed. The social dimension of human existence was repressed, and greed, acquisitiveness and competitiveness denied fellowship both among men and among nations. As a matter of fact man attains true freedom *within* society, in intrinsic relation to it, and not as its officious observer or its serf. The integration of personal freedom and society is therefore also a realization of the intregal person of man.

We live and are active in Time, even though Time is merciless in its attitude toward man and oppresses him from every side. We are called upon to overcome the tormenting contradictions of Time and to fulfil our historic destiny. To do so is, as it were, an act of horizontal self-transcendence (as distinct from the vertical one to God), and yet it is that only in so far as it does justice to the self in its initial and ultimate freedom. Man's relation to and awareness of Nature and History must then be born of freedom, although in fact he is, more often than not, servile toward them, while they, by their hidden power, crush him for the purpose of gaining their own ends. Some are so impressed by the shattering forces of History or so naïve as to decline altogether to bear the burden of their historic responsibility.[1]

History is a call to man's freedom, and it is sustained in freedom, in which he is conscious of and communicates with other selves. He is brought face to face with the challenge of unique and irrevocable situations; and it is freedom that makes him share, understand, espouse, rather than observe them indifferently or collaborate officiously with them. Only thus they cease to be a confused series of mere incidental happenings to be remembered or forgotten. History is, in fact, being fulfilled by man's will to be contemporaneous with History and by his readiness to treat it autobiographically. Every objectification of

---

[1] An American statesman quoted by Rosenstock-Huessy (op. cit.) exclaimed: 'Happy is the country that has no History. America has not much of it, and should try to have even less.' A fitting exemplification of George Eliot's dictum: 'The happiest women, like the happiest nations, have no History!' Mr. Ford endorses the statement by proclaiming in a witness box: 'History is bunk!'

The Beginning and the End

History, every attitude of mere extraneous aloofness towards it, is a betrayal both of History and of freedom, and brings its penalty of invading and possessing man and hence destroying, dehumanizing human life.

The freedom of man, then, involves all these things: it reveals his supreme responsibility for himself and for his life. But such responsibility is falsified by mere possession of oneself: it is fulfilled in self-transcendence, from beyond the self, as well as in self-communication with other men, in self-identification with the rest of mankind in all the awfulness and greatness of its historical, national, social, political and cultural destiny.

(d) Man in Estrangement

Karl Marx made an extremely important discovery about the place of man in History and in the world which, at the time, exceedingly surprised and even shocked the economists. Its relevance is now more evident than ever before. We shall devote a few pages to this Marxian insight not only in the belief that it throws new light on the subject in hand, viz. the problem of human freedom, but, in addition, with the avowed aim of dispelling certain current notions about Marx's conception of man which are a travesty of his real views and seem to have made disreputable one who is more profoundly a prophet of true Christian humanism than many of its official advocates.[1] The

---

[1] One cannot help noting the extremely and painfully onesided characterization of Marxist Communism in *Divini Redemptoris* of Pius XI—doubly painful coming as it does from one of the greatest and most enlightened Roman pontiffs: Communism, 'the satanic scourge' (!), which is said to be based on the doctrine that 'there is in the world only one reality, matter, the blind forces of which evolve into plant, animal, and man', 'strips man of his liberty . . . robs human personality of all its dignity, and removes all the moral restraints that check the eruptions of blind impulse (?). Since, according to Communism, human personality is, so to say, a mere wheel in the machine of the universe, the natural rights which spring from it are denied to individuals and attributed to the community. . . . Refusing to human duties any sacred character, such a doctrine logically makes marriage and the family a purely artificial . . . institution.' (?) Society based on Marxist tenets is further described as having 'only one mission: the production of material things by means of collective labour' and as 'leading to an era which is the result of blind evolutionary processes'. In short, 'a system full of errors and illusions . . . subverting the social order, because it means the destruction of its foundations, . . . because it has no sense of the rights, dignity, and liberty of human personality, . . . or of moral responsibility' (!) (*Div. Red.* 9–12; 23).

fact that he stood under the sign of atheism is largely a matter for Christians to congratulate themselves on and does not detract anything from the fact that Marxism is intrinsically related to the truths of Christianity.

Marx's fundamental work, *Das Kapital*, the ostensible aim of which is to discover the laws governing capitalist society, is in fact an introduction to anthropology, to the doctrine of man. In his analysis of the conflicts and contradictions inherent in social life Marx points to the presence of certain 'illusions' which constantly beset men. These illusions, which ultimately result in the disintegration of human existence, issue from what he calls 'estrangement' or 'alienation'. 'Estrangement' is a division within man who, having created certain symbols and institutions, ceases to recognize them as the products of his activity and comes to live under the impression that they are things or objects extraneous to and independent of his human nature and, finally, inaccessible to human influence. When we project an ideal outside the concrete relations of human life, or, more specifically, of human society, we are no more subjects but objects and even victims of our objectifications.

The most striking evidence of the phenomenon of estrangement is taken from the domain of labour. An artisan who remains throughout an active subject in his creative work will continue to be master of his productive activity, engaging his personality and freedom in it. The wage-earner on the other hand, is being dispossessed alike of the instruments and products of his work, and hence dispossessed of himself. What he produces turns into 'things' and 'goods', into impersonal abstractions, thus signifying their alienation from him. Hence proceeds Marx's famous critique of capitalism as a system of commodity production in which labour power itself has become a commodity, bought and sold in the market like any other object of exchange; a system involving the concentration of the ownership of the means of production in the hands of a minority class, and the emergence of a class of propertyless persons who must exist by selling their labour. [1]

Owing to these conditions work assumes the character of a crushing necessity which may or may not cover the material needs of the life of the worker but takes away its real value. It

[1] Marx gives a searching analysis of this process of disintegration and depersonalization in his *Economic and Philosophical Manuscripts*.

does not constitute any more an inherent part of his existence and instead of revealing denies and suppresses his manhood. Work ceases to be a free activity which testifies to man's creative nature and becomes forced labour or paid enslavement. 'All estrangement', says Marx, 'means the loss of human dignity.'[1] Man shall not be alienated from the things he makes or uses, else he will become their slave. And even if he were to engage his whole personality, his initiative, his creative imagination, the values thereby created will remain external to him if his contribution is to be measured in terms of impersonal commodities or capital employed in buying labour-force (wages). The more values are thus created, the more the employer will tend to accumulate his 'variable capital' at the expense of those who bear the 'curse of labour', and the more the worker is rendered dependent on the capital which dispossesses him every day of the products of his creativity and thus of his humanity.[2] 'It is by alienated labour that man creates not only hostile relations between himself and the object, between himself and the act of production, but also hostile relations between himself and other persons. As he works to his own detriment and creates things which do not belong to him, he establishes by his own productivity and the things he makes the sovereignty of those who do not create. While his own activity alienates him from himself, another takes possession of it, though in fact it does not pertain to him. The relation which exists between the worker and his work issues in the relations which exist between the capitalist and the labourer.'[3]

The determining factor in this evaluation of human work is

[1] Lenin remarked that Marx called for the struggle of a better order of society 'in the name of the real human personality' (*Frederick Engels*). It is noteworthy that even fervent admirers of the capitalist system perceive in its inward logic a process of depersonalization. Joseph Schumpeter's *Capitalism, Socialism and Democracy*, a story told with nostalgia and bitterness, shows how capitalism destroys itself in the concentration of production in the hands of an ever smaller number of giant combines. Social and economic processes become depersonalized; even the idea of property is rendered hollow and dead with the rise of bonds and shares.

[2] This does not mean, of course, that the labour in the capitalist society is wasted or that the things produced are not useful or beautiful, and that the only thing to do is to stop making them. Marxism is very far from the romantic dreams of some late nineteenth-century socialists about unperturbed rural existence dependent on handicraft: it accepts the challenge of and speaks to a world of demonic technocracy.

[3] *Economic and Philosophical Manuscripts.*

manifestly not the alleged mere economic necessity but a moral and spiritual motive. Nobody, indeed, before Marx had shown so clearly the spiritual role of productive agencies in human History.

The horror of man's moral as well as material estrangement is seen most clearly in the power of money over his brain and heart. 'That which exists for me by means of money, that which can be paid for, that is to say, that which money can bring about, I am that very thing, I, the owner of money. My force is as great as the force of money. The virtues of money are my virtues and my power: the virtues of him who possesses it. What I am and what I can do is in no way determined by my person. I am ugly, but I can buy myself the most beautiful woman: thus I am no more ugly, for the effect, the abhorrence of ugliness is made void by money. . . . I am an evil man, dishonest, conscienceless, spiritless; but money is honoured, and so he who possesses it is likewise honoured. Money is the greatest good, and so he who owns it is also good. Money, to tell the truth, even spares me the pain of being honest: it is presumed that I am honest. I am devoid of spirit, but money is the true spirit of all things: how then can its owner be without spirit? Is he not able to buy his 'spiritual men'? Is not he who has the power over spiritual men more spiritual than the most spiritual among them? I who, thanks to money, am capable of attaining all that to which man's heart aspires, am I not in possession of all human values? My money, does it not transform all my insufficiencies into their opposite? If money is the link which attaches me to human life, to society, to nature and to man, is it not the link of all links? Can it not join and sunder all links? But is it not therefore also the source of all division? . . . Shakespeare discerns two main characteristics in money: 1. It is the visible deity, the conversion of all human and natural virtues into their contrary, the universal confusion and falsification of values. . . . 2. It is the universal prostitute, the world-wide go-between among men and nations.'[1]

Man, then, alienates his own creations, or is forced to do so, from himself, and thereupon submits to them—such is the fundamental law of estrangement which threatens human existence at every step: in social relationships, in cultural activities, in science, in technology and even in religion. In the instances

[1] Op. cit.

already noted at the beginning of this essay we have seen that philosophical Idealism exhibits a similar tendency to estrangement, whereby man is divorced from History and his historic destiny.

The question as to whether the Marxian critique of estrangement can be sustained on materialist assumptions is disputable;[1] so is the question as to whether it can be sustained on 'collectivist' grounds.[2] At any rate it has shown one most important

---

[1] It hardly needs saying that Marxist materialism has nothing in common with the peculiar doctrine that 'it's all a question of glandular secretion'. Too much of one gland, too little of another—and you get your *Ninth Symphony*, or your *Hamlet*, or your *Gioconde*. As a matter of fact, Marxism repudiates even mere economic materialism. 'It is not that the economic position is the *cause* and *alone active*, while everything else only has a passive effect' (Engels, *Letter to Heinz Starkenburg*. Italics in the original). 'If somebody twists our argument about the dependence of History on the production and reproduction of life into the statement that the economic element is the *only* determining one, he transforms it into a meaningless, abstract and absurd phrase. . . . Political, legal, philosophical theories, religious ideas . . . also exercise their influence upon the course of the historical struggles and in many cases preponderate in determining their form' (Engels, *Letter to Joseph Bloch*). Engels goes on to say that he and Marx are themselves partly to blame for the fact that some Marxists 'lay more stress on the economic side than is due to it. We had to emphasize this principle in opposition to our adversaries, who denied it, and we had not always the time, the place or the opportunity to allow the other elements involved to come into their rights. . . . And I cannot exempt many of the more recent "Marxists" from this reproach, for the most wonderful rubbish has been produced from this quarter' (ibid.). If Marxism stipulates that 'in the interaction of various elements in human life the economic one asserts itself as the decisive one' (Engels), this presents above all a description of a factual state of affairs; and human life bears out amply the Marxian analysis. Marx has merely stripped off the moral and religious pretexts that cover this state of affairs and shown it in its horrifying nakedness.

[2] 'Collectivism', as implied in Marx's strictures of estrangement, can surely mean only one thing: that man is fundamentally a 'relational' being, or, as it were, a trans-subjective being, while society is not an aggregate of individual human units, but a macrocosmos co-extensive with man. From the point of view of practical ethics this means that individual actions are 'not enough'. It is not enough for the serf-owner to be personally kind to his serfs, or for the benevolent rich to distribute old clothes to the victims of the system they represent. Tolstoy said: 'I sit on a man's back, choking him and making him carry me, and yet assure myself and others that I am very sorry for him and wish to ease his lot by all possible means—except by getting off his back' (*What then Must We Do?*). The individual altruistic virtues must acquire another dimension, that of social responsibility. Freedom, in this connection, implies a passing beyond one's personal judgment and behaviour into the 'collective', or rather the community. Without taking this seriously into account it is impossible to meet the question as to what to do in the case of a moral conflict between the individual and society. We may add, by the way, that if freedom means the possibility of speculating, on a

and even decisive fact concerning man: it has shown that the consciousness he has of himself does not always correspond to what he truly is. Life, and particularly social life, with all its inherent contradictions of which Marx was more aware than most of his predecessors, Christian or otherwise, is pregnant with illusions: some values appear to us as having an origin, a reality, a development wholly extraneous to us, and we constantly fall under the sway of their crushing objectivity; whereas in fact these values are we ourselves, our very existence.

If we consider the true philosophical implications of the Marxian theory of 'values' and 'surplus values', as it is expounded in *Das Kapital*, we are driven to acknowledge that it pertains not only to the limited sphere of political economy: it represents one of the greatest contributions to ethics—a contribution which, through its 'inversion' or humanization of social and economic values, exhibits, more than the innumerable smart ethical systems with their inquests into the 'deep moral causes' of human behaviour, the true significance of man as endowed with freedom and called upon to create and humanize the world in which he lives and his relationships with other men. 'The materialist doctrine', says Marx in the Third Thesis on Feuerbach, 'that men are products of circumstances and upbringing and that, therefore, changed men are products of other circumstances and changed upbringing forgets that circumstances are changed precisely by men, and that the eductaor must himself be educated. Hence this doctrine necessarily arrives at dividing society into two parts, of which one towers above society.'

Marx identifies freedom and creativity: freedom is the creation of oneself and of the world. With man's creative action begins the process of human History which transcends the realm of nature, of purely physical laws and of biological evolution, while yet relating History to that realm. We are far removed here from Materialism in the vulgar sense of the term which subjects men to the immutable laws of external nature, or, for

large or small scale, of levying tribute on one's fellow-men, or of deliberately destroying precious necessary commodities to keep the prices up, which activities parade sometimes under the name of 'private initiative', we may safely decline to pay homage to such a freedom without betraying true freedom. Under Christian 'law' (as distinct from Roman Law) man is the steward of his possessions. He administers them not only for his own profit but above all as responsible to God and to other men.

the matter of that, isolates them from the world and from one another. It is a Materialism which involves a self-transcendence as well as communion, a *Miteinandersein* in freedom, to use a favourite term of modern Existentialism: in fact, it is a very questionable Materialism. . . . 'The whole of History is nothing but a continuous free transformation of nature by man' (*The Poverty of Philosophy*). In this continuous creativity the scope and meaning of human freedom finds expression; and this betrays the fact that the essence of Marx's commonwealth is not only to be a material kingdom, but one to be born of and guided by the power of man's creative spirit.

'What is freedom?' asks Marx in his *The Jewish Question*.[1] 'According to the Declaration of the Rights of Man of 1791 freedom consists "à pouvoir faire tout ce que ne nuit pas à autrui". The limits in which everyone can move without being a nuisance to another are fixed by law, just as the limit between two fields is fixed by a picket. We are concerned here with the freedom of man viewed as an isolated entity left to itself. . . . Man's right and freedom are based not on the relations between man and man, but rather on the division between them. It is the right and freedom of this division, the right of the individual limited by itself.'

'The practical application of this liberty is the right of private property. What is however this latter right? "Le droit de pro-priété est celui qui appartient a tout citoyen de jouir et de dis-poser à son gré de ses biens, de ses revenues, du fruit de son travail et de son industrie" (1793 Constitution). The right of property is thus the right to enjoy one's fortune and dispose of it according to one's inclinations irrespective of other men, inde-pendently of the community: it is the right of selfishness. And it is the application of this individualistic liberty that provides the basis for bourgeois society. It makes every man see in the other man not the realization but the limitation of his free-dom.'[2]

'None of the alleged rights of man transcends, therefore, the egotistic man—man as member of bourgeois society, that is to

[1] See *Deutsch-Franzoesische Jahrbuecher*.

[2] Lenin exclaimed later with his usual cynical frankness: 'Freedom? For what?' A blasphemy, perhaps. But a man blasphemes only when he has loved that at which he sneers, only where he has believed. We are driven to admit that in a life dominated by money freedom is a snare and a delusion.

say, an individual divorced from the community, relying on itself, solely preoccupied with its private interest and obeying the promptings of its private arbitrary will. . . . The only link which binds men together is the natural necessity, the private need and interest, the conservation of their respective properties and of egotism in others. . . . But this man is an abstraction and an artificiality: . . . he is not man but an abstract citizen.'

We have quoted this lengthy passage, since it presents both a powerful critique of the betrayal of freedom by 'alienated' bourgeois society and Marx's insight into a fundamental aspect of man's freedom.

(e) The Theology of Freedom

What we have tried to state in the chapter on freedom in somewhat abstract philosophical terms must now be restated in more concrete, theological language.

'And God said, Let us make man in our image, after our likeness. . . . So God created man in His own image, in the image of God created He him' (Gen. i, 26–7). Such is the witness of revelation and such is the deepest intuition of the creature about its true nature. 'Thou hidest Thy face, they are troubled: Thou takest away their breath, they die and return to the dust. Thou sendest forth Thy Spirit, they are created; and Thou renewest the face of the earth' (Ps. civ, 29–30).

How are we to reconcile the fact of man's creatureliness and hence his utter dependence on the Creator with that of his freedom whose very nature is 'to be oneself', independent, ungoverned, uncaused, 'original', autonomous? To discuss, or indeed to pose, this question may appear a proposterous undertaking: 'O man, who art thou that repliest against God? Shall the thing formed say to him that formed it, why hast thou made me thus?' And yet insight into the transcendence of the origin of all things permits, or even drives us with commanding power, to look for and to understand the ultimate, original correlation between our life and that wholly other life which is God's.

It was Nicolas Hartmann's contention that human freedom is incompatible with the existence of God, and he establishes a series of antinomies which purport to show that a fundamental contradiction exists between the ethical world-view based on man's free realization of ideal values and the religious con-

sciousness based on man's dependence on a divine being (see his *Ethics*, vol. iii, ch. 21, ff., English translation). How can man be free, he asks, as against the principle to which as man he ought to be subject? In other words, if God is almighty, his ultimate ends must needs be the determinants of man's existence and, consequently, annul his (man's) freedom and self-determination. Hartmann concludes that the idea of God is a supremely immoral idea, and he rejects it for the sake of human dignity, freedom, and creativeness.

Hartmann's atheism raises a very real problem, for the free being of man is threatened not only from the side of Nature which can be and is being modelled by men, but also, and even primarily, by the assertions of an abstract divine absolutism which attempt to deduce logically from God's eternal decrees the mysterious pathways of human destiny. Hartmann presents, moreover, a powerful challenge to a religious conception of freedom according to which man is the servant of a divine moral law who is responsible for fulfilling or not fulfilling it and thus rewarded or punished respectively. In point of fact freedom is not a mere device conceived by God to vindicate the idea of punishment and of reward, nor is it a formal freedom *from* something, a mere *liberum arbitrium indifferentiae*, but the fundamental condition of the *reciprocal* relation between God and man. Man is free in relation to God not only in the sense that he is endowed with a capacity to turn towards God or away from Him (which is evidence of determination, since, presumably, if the external factor is lacking the will does not choose, and if it does choose it is determined to do so and hence in a sense disfranchised), but that he is called upon to *create*, to bring forth in freedom new values, to introduce purpose into the world, to transform the world.[1] He is called upon to transform the world in prayer and in thought, in art and in craftsmanship, in technology and in science, and even in politics, seeing that creative politics become and are an urgent necessity and demand of human existence. In short, man is called upon to *co-operate with God*. Such co-operation has little

[1] St. Maximus the Confessor who has devoted much attention to the problem of freewill in the context of Christological controversies perceives in the freedom of choice (he calls it θέλημα γνωμικόν) a manifest limitation and imperfection since it implies a determination from without; whereas true freedom (θέλημα φυσικόν) knows no such limitation since it is determined entirely from within and is in no need of choosing an extraneous object.

or nothing in common with 'good works' by which man believes himself able to merit, or to cash in on, the grace of God. There is no merit, supererogatory or otherwise, before God. Rather, man's creatorship is his inward destiny in which God acts and lives—the creative representation of divine 'energies' in which God's redeeming, sanctifying power is carried into the world. Such a creative representation is beyond any reckoning or compensation, nor can it be expressed in terms of legal fictions by which man is alleged to gain a certitude of being justified before the judgment of a heavenly divine tribunal. The creative activity of man is the response to a call by virtue of which he shares in the unceasing creative operation of God.

True, the creative act of man also involves an element of tragedy: it is, in a sense, bound up with his wretched and impotent condition; it is, like Plato's Eros, a child of two parents, Penia and Poros, of poverty and wealth, of insufficiency, disquietude and longing for fulfilment as well as of bounteousness, plenitude and liberality. Man is never alone or solely related to himself in his creatorship; rather, he is engaged in a dialogue, in an activity kindled by the nuptial fire of Hymen. He is addressed by, he responds to, he meets and inter-acts with, his other One, with God, with other men, with angels or demons, and, indeed, with other things, which thereby lose their character of thinghood and become his inmost life. In all these inter-relations man is both active and passive. And yet all human creativity brings with it something new, something that was not there before, in other words, something that is part of creative divine-human fulfilment.

Hartmann is right in his defence of man's creative vocation as against a religious world-view for which freedom is merely a condition of obeying a 'divine law' or the 'will of God'; but he, together with the many theological parties to the dispute, is wrong in failing to see that in actual fact it is the fundamental affirmation of Christian theism that man is endowed with the image of the Creator and is, therefore, himself creator. His freedom has scope both over the regularity (or apparent regularity) of Nature with her various determinations, and as regards the setting up of ends which pertain to the divine-human sphere of God's creative and providential order. The Christian revelation shows God not as an abstract idea of the good which, in relation to man, inevitably appears in the shape of norms and laws,

imperilling, as they do, his (man's) freedom, but as a living person who calls man to share in his creative activity, who desires man's participation in his creatorship and, in doing so, voluntarily limits his own absolute freedom, i.e. the very thing which is a condition of his existence. Such is the real meaning of the much misunderstood and misinterpreted doctrine of 'synergism' (a term which owes its origin to Scripture), particularly characteristic of Eastern Orthodox theology: a doctrine which refuses to affirm human freedom without reference to divine freedom or to affirm divine freedom without reference to human freedom, and thus gives the lie both to Pelagian moralism and to Augustinian monism.

Sergius Bulgakov, in a remarkable study entitled *Judas the Traitor Apostle*,[1] has expressed the idea that the creation of man includes not only a unilateral call into existence on the part of God but also, as it were, a response, a simultaneous self-establishment of the free creature, a consent of the human self to its establishment by God. Man accepts his creaturehood in freedom and freely shares in his making. It is here that we must seek the clue for the mysterious character of human destiny. The creation of the self cannot but be a call to *self*-creation, to a free self-determination, for, as we have already seen, this is of the very essence of the self. Man participates in the divine act of his own creation; to be more precise, God makes man share in his divine creative act. To be created by God is no mere passive createdness or obedience to the divine call into existence but includes also the creature's own response and consent to be. Such is the abundance of the love of God that he limits his own absoluteness and passes on his creative will to the creature. Indeed, the very fact of God's love reveals the self-determination of every self other than himself, every other-one over against God, who is converted by his love and wisdom into destined existence. God creates man through man himself. Man is a subject: he is not and cannot be an object at any one point of his existence, and his freedom arises freely and in freedom. The Christian Father who has probably penetrated most deeply to the root of this problem is Gregory of Nyssa who boldly asserts that the spirit of man is not 'given' ($\delta\acute{\epsilon}\delta\omega\kappa\epsilon\nu$) to him in creation

---

[1] The study is devoted to a searching analysis and interpretation of the story of the mysterious and demonic companion of Jesus Christ who epitomizes the riddle and ultimate tragedy of fallen and yet divinely-chosen man.

Theodicy

but that God makes man 'participate ($\mu\epsilon\tau\epsilon\delta\omega\kappa\epsilon\nu$) in his creator-ship.[1]

But, Fr. Bulgakov argues, the human creature utters its free consent to the call of God into being, not in the abstract, but concretely, that is to say, it consents to a distinct, concrete individual vocation. God does not create people who differ from one another by their numbers, rather he creates distinct persons with unique and unrepeatable destinies. It is thus that each and every free human being is an end in itself, having his own place to fill and his own purpose to fulfil—a fountain from the Unknown coming into the world to live his own life. God's creation becomes effective in that the human self confronts itself primordially in the power of its freedom and accepts the divine challenge to life. But the manner of this acceptance brings with it peculiar features or 'themes' into the life of man, and all the abysmal consequences which this primordial relationship with God must have for him. In other words, the original choice of man implies all the concrete manifestations which characterize his actual living.[2] 'Thine eyes did see my substance, yet being unperfect; in thy book all my members were written, which in continuance were fashioned, when as yet there was none of them' (Ps. cxxxix, 16).

These ideas raise a series of important problems and also difficulties which are, so far as Fr. Bulgakov's position is concerned, enhanced by his tendency to range himself on the side of the Kantian idea of 'intelligible freedom'.[3] If, we may argue, human life is primordially fixed by an original act of choice, are we not faced with a form of predestination (as it were, a human or divine-human in contra-distinction to the traditional divine predestination), whereby the free activity of man as we know him in his concrete existence loses its decisive character? What can be the meaning of the historical process if all things are already determined in an initial instantaneous choice? What meaning can be attached on these premises to the historical future? These questions can be met by stating that the 'original choice' is, so to speak, the prototype to which human life

[1] *De hominis opificio*, c. ix. Elsewhere he speaks of the free creature's 'emancipation' ($\dot{\omega}s$ $\alpha\dot{\upsilon}\tau o\kappa\rho\alpha\tau o\rho\iota\kappa\dot{\eta}$ $\tau\iota s$ $\alpha\dot{\upsilon}\theta\epsilon\nu\tau\epsilon\acute{\iota}a$) by virtue of which, it becomes 'its own parent' ($\dot{\epsilon}\alpha\upsilon\tau\omega\nu$ $\pi\alpha\tau\acute{\epsilon}\rho\epsilon s$), *De vita Moysis, I.*

[2] See also Bulgakov's *The Burning Bush*, where this is developed with particular reference to the doctrine of Original Sin.

[3] See above the discussion of the Kantian view of Time.

approximates, and, at the same time, the end or goal to which it may be said to aspire; in other words, we may answer in terms of the two aspects under which Plato conceives of Forms or Ideas. But this leads inevitably to a dualistic Idealism, which we have explicitly repudiated on account of its inherent devaluation or even negation of Time and History. The point at issue, it would seem, can only be met by affirming that all the free acts of man pertaining to his historical existence are implied and involved in a unique, *temporal as well as supra-temporal*, act of self-determination and gradually, even if very unevenly, unfold themselves in a series of crisis-events in the course of his living. The 'original choice' is not aloof or apart, projected on to the stage of our historical existence, making this latter a 'foregone conclusion': rather, it is the innermost core of human existence, not only in the sense of a 'constitutive principle' but also, by virtue of its actualization in Time, in the sense of a *Beginning* pressing towards fulfilment, which is inconceivable except in relation to an *End*. It is thus that Time is not reduced to a mere accident in the eternal drama of heaven and the movements of Time, which are informed by the exercise of man's freedom, retain their full significance and decisiveness for his eternal destiny. The problem is similar to that with which we had to deal in the discussion of the relation between the two aspects underlying the conception of the End as already present and yet as coming to be.

It is evident that these tentative suggestions do not resolve all the difficulties of the problem in hand. But we have agreed that the supply of ready-made solutions is very limited, not only on account of the limitations of the human mind but also because reality itself does not bear such solutions.

One thing emerges clearly from this discussion: namely, that freedom cannot be spoken of as 'made' by God, unless we are prepared to do violence to the fundamental and distinctive character of freedom. It is more accurate to say that God sets freedom as the condition of his creative act; in other words, freedom is no mere product of creation, or the 'effect' of a 'cause', but, as it were, creation itself, the original divine-human act of creativity.

It is impossible to introduce at this stage the classic distinction of man, endowed with the 'liberty of the sons of God', or man in the state of 'original justice', and the unjustified sinner

divested of such liberty, for this very distinction is meaningful only on the assumption of the ultimate freedom which underlies any predicates which man, as we know him, possesses. God's very act of calling man into being is realized in and implies an act of self-initiation on the part of man, since man's being is to be free throughout, and it cannot be affected by any mere extraneous operation or compulsion, albeit that of almighty God himself. But each and every act of such self-initiation and freedom is at the same time an intrinsic witness to man's supreme relatedness to God.

We do not postulate an ontological dualism in describing freedom in these terms: we do not, that is to say, in any way imply the existence of another being 'added on to' or claiming equality with God. What we mean to say is that creation is an act in which God's absolute priority never annuls human freedom as an original source of action, and that, while belonging to a wholly other order of being, God yet enters into a positive relation with the creature in its coming to be, in its being and becoming. Dualism, no less than monism, both of which attempt to reconcile God's creatorship and the creature's freedom, are mere abstract metaphysical propositions: they do not so much as point to the heart of the mystery of freedom. For freedom is a true *Grenzbegriff*, a 'limiting notion', beyond the reach of conceptual reasoning, and it can be described, as we have tried to do, only in mythological language, that is, the language of revelation.

If freedom is what we think it to be we may be able to have a glimpse into the meaning of the tragedy of human life. What does God's bountiful will signify in face of the immeasurable sufferings and torments of existence? Such was the original concern of theodicy. We cannot be too slow in answering the question, for in these matters 'the Why persists in laughing at all possible Becauses'. Nevertheless we are compelled to say that God's will is no extraneous fate, no 'divine will' disposing insuperably and irresistibly of his creatures, no rational order of things or rational teleological activity in this 'best of all possible worlds'. Were it that, we had better refuse to accept this or any other world for better or for worse. We are not convinced by the comforters of Job, in whatever garb, with their reassuring providentialism or their 'applied morals and religion', and we decline the honour of being fitted in into a reasonable and expedient scheme of things. God is in no need of our reasonable-

ness, and, evidently, there is more truth in Job's accusations against God than in all the theodicies provided by his friends: 'Who is it that darkeneth counsel by words without understanding' (Job xxxviii, 2).

We shall have to concern ourselves more fully later on with the fact of God's providence in the world and in History; we may, however, anticipate the subject here by saying that it presents a chain of mysteries in heaven and on earth—events which, though they are decisive happenings in Time, are not really happenings of Time alone. They take us back to the dawn of being, to the first and last boundary of our existence which is beyond Time and yet in Time and for Time: to that primordial day of creation when out of the depth of the void there resounds the creature's free response to the divine call into being. Every human destiny has its mysterious prologue in heaven where man chooses to be himself. Man *freely* consents to the pathways of his destiny, even though it be full of darkness, bitterness and torment. This freedom may imbue life with that terrible character which compels so many to doubt the existence of providence and to conclude that the whole of History is a refutation of it. The triumph of evil over the good would seem indeed irreconcilable with the existence of providence. But it is precisely the tragic nature of historical destiny which evinces the mystery of freedom as the source of that tragedy to which divine necessity and constraint could easily put an end. Such constraint, however, would contradict the very essence of God's relation to man and of man's relation to God. In the world of boundless horrors, in its immeasurable chasms, there sounds the untold voice of man, a creative whisper, a mysterious *let it be*, that is, the creature's free choice and desire to be itself, to be what it actually is. And God draws this human voice into his own creative call, receives it into his own transcendent act of creativity and thus designates the infinitely multiple content of human life. In truth, it is a fearful thing to fall into the hands of the living God, for *he gives everyone what his soul has willed and desired.* Such is the mystery of divine *and* human providence, of divine-human providence and divine-human foreordination.

(f) *Mysterium Iniquitatis*

The doctrine of the Fall and of original sin (which, in the

language of Christian mythology, refers to the transgression of the first man in paradise, extending in its effects to his descendants and to the whole human race) has a direct bearing on the problem of theodicy. We have undertaken to listen to this problem since we all belong to those to whom the Cross is a stumbling block and a foolishness. 'If God is righteous, it is mooted, how can we reconcile this fact with the fatal consequences of a sin that we have not committed and for which we cannot, therefore, be held responsible?'

We shall not discuss here the difficulties which are involved in an ill-conceived doctrine of original sin based on a false and abstract dissolution of mankind into separate, extraneously related individuals. What we intend to show is that original sin refers not to the disturbance of a pre-established harmony, nor even to the transgression of a divine law in the face of which neither the sacred Mysteries, nor repentance nor prayer would avail, but to the fact that our divided state cannot be rightly estimated except in connexion with man's ultimate personal relation to God.

The doctrine of original sin points to the fact that in the very depth of the human spirit resides a tendency which betrays his manhood, which exposes him to the forces of disintegration and belies his true destiny. To ascribe this betrayal to the progenitor of mankind in an original evil act is to see it as an event at the ultimate boundary of human existence, in the depth of free self-determination on the part of man over against God. Man's free consent to creation is followed by another original act of freedom, that of revolt and hostility towards God. In other words, the nature of the Fall is not to be defined primarily with reference to external conditions, legal or otherwise, but to the deepest dimensions of man's being.

For many centuries Christian thought has helplessly wrestled with the question as to what is original sin, as to where and when it occurred. This question drove Origen into the pitfalls of pre-existentialism (*creatio ab aeterno*) which attempts to explain the unknown by the unknown and unaccountably assumes men's previous existence in order to understand their present one. It has prompted others to build up the weakly theory of arbitrary imputation (*imputatio*) of the sin of the human progenitors to their posterity or, as we believe, the equally unconvincing Augustinian and scholastic theory—not to be found in Christian

teaching before the fourth century and wrongly attributed to St. Paul—according to which God already divests man of 'supernatural' grace at his birth, as a consequence of which man is born in sin.[1]

It is meaningless to speak of sin as belonging to Adam alone while we are merely its unwilling casualties, for sin (whether 'original', or 'habitual' or 'actual'), as every other act of freedom, involves personal responsibility and cannot in the last resort be subject to any laws of causality or fate. It is not by chance that the Greeks conceived of tragedy as bound up with the idea of hereditary guilt and vengeance and with the idea of retribution for a crime committed unwittingly (Oedipus), the reason being that they lacked the sense of personality. We are aware, however, of some profound guilt in us involving our whole being: not of sins but of *sin*, of that warring of the will against the good, of that 'other law' which 'dwelleth in my members' and leads me to 'the evil which I would not that I do' (Rom. vii, 18-24).[2] This very real, even if inarticulate, consciousness of some initial self-determination to evil is a mark of our personal sharing in the original sin of Adam, which however, we may add, must not be interpreted in juridical terms involving formal liability to punishment. 'Not Adam alone but with him each and everyone of us committed or commits for himself Adam's sin, which is, therefore, our own sin, that is, a deed of our will and not of our unwillingness.'[3] Adam's sin is thus not simply one sin amongst others—a first sin pertaining to a first human individual called Adam. It is a unique sin, which is, as it were, the

---

[1] To be more precise, this latter theory declares that the qualities, known in scholasticism as Adam's supernatural splendours of original perfection with its perfect sanctity and perfect intellectual ability (which, as distinct from *pura naturalia*, represents a *donum superadditum*) were forfeited by him through sin. As a consequence of this Adam began 'the process of sinful motion' which drags the whole human race into its flow and consists in concupiscence and subsequent generation (see, e.g., St. Thomas Aqu., *De malo*, qu. 4)

[2] Cf. the strikingly similar witness of the pagan Ovidius:
video meliora, proboque
deteriora sequor.
The discoveries of the modern psychoanalysts and the analogous prognostications in the sphere of sociology (Marx) and ethics (Nietzsche, Dostoevsky) point to similar experiences. . . . We must, however, be on guard against the current distasteful attitude of triumph among Christian apologists and devout ecclesiastics wherever and whenever a scientist, or a man of letters, or a statesman bestows his blessings on religious truths.

[3] See the already cited *The Burning Bush* by S. Bulgakov (ch. ii, passim).

metaphysical ground of all other sins: it is *the* sin of man's free-dom—a primordial evil self-determination of man. It stands beyond the limits of an individual human existence, to be more precise, at the very limit of human existence, on the threshold of life. Adam sinned originally not as 'Adam', or not only as such, but as everyone does. In other words, Adam, in commit-ting original sin, did so as a real, not a juridical, representative of mankind: he did so as everyone would do and in fact does; and the story of his and Eve's fall is the true story of humanity and what has been its ruin in every individual case. All are equal and co-inhere in the sin originally committed; and what befell the 'first man' has happened to man *per se*, to our very manhood.[1]

The Church has repudiated Origen's teaching about the pre-existence of the human soul, because this teaching was closely bound up with the Neoplatonic interpretation of the world's origin, and conceived of creation as a falling away, *katabole*, from God, or, so far as man is concerned, as a falling away of the human soul from the world of eternal Spirit. The *pre*-existence of human souls without bodies or before embodiment, indeed, openly contradicts the Christian conception of man as an incar-

---

[1] 'La personne humaine n'est pas une partie de l'être humain, comme les personnes de la Trinité ne sont pas des parties de Dieu. C'est pourquoi la qualité de l'image de Dieu ne revient pas à un élément quelconque du composé humain, mais se réfère à toute la nature de l'homme dans son inté-grité. Le premier homme qui contenait en lui toute la nature humaine était aussi la personne unique. "Car le nom d'Adam—dit saint Grégoire de Nysse—n'est pas donné maintenant à l'objet créé, comme dans les récits qui suivent. Mais l'homme créé n'a pas un nom particulier, il est l'homme uni-versel. Donc, par cette désignation universelle de la nature, nous sommes invités à comprendre que la Providence et Puissance divines embrassent tout le genre humain dans la première création . . . Car l'image n'est pas dans une partie de la nature, ni la grace dans un individu parmi ceux qu'il regarde, mais c'est sur la race toute entière que cette vertu s'étend" . . .' (V. Lossky, *Essai sur la Théologie Mystique de l'Eglise d'Orient*, p. 115).

The co-inherence of mankind in its fallen as well as original and redeemed state is a recurring theme in the works of Charles Williams (see, e.g., his novels *Descent into Hell* and *Many Dimensions*). It would seem that one of the principle features of contemporary literature is its insight into a human world under the dominion of sin and death. This is true not only of the 'pessimistic humanism' of a Proust or Miller but, above all, of such writers as Joyce, Kafka, Mauriac, Sartre and, among the earlier Russian novelists, of course, Dostoevsky for whom the strickenness of man is no mere division, known since Shakespeare, but a polarity, a longing for the greatest holiness and purity and, along with this, a longing for what is terrifyingly base. They know that in speaking of wounded humanity they are speaking of the deadly reality of sin, not of a theological ogre. But they do not moralize.

nate spirit or a spiritual body. There is not and cannot be any other time that precedes the Time of human existence. Man arises in and with the creative act of God, although he be a child of Eternity as well as of Time. But such repudiation of pre-existence in Time by no means excludes the possibility of an event that occurs at the limit or boundary of Time. God creates man according to His image and likeness—not, however, as we have seen, in the sole power of His almightiness but in His creature's freedom, in virtue of which it shares in, and consents to, this creative act. Every human soul, therefore, lives by its will to live. The boundary of Time in which—by an act of divine-human creativity—the creature is called into being is also the existential point at which everyone actualizes for himself and freely his partnership in, though he does not 'repeat', Adam's original sin and hence his solidarity with our stricken, sinful world.

We may ask why the soul does not know or remember this primal act of self-determination against God, this primordial consent to sinful existence? Is it not simply a mystifying invention of the speculative human brain? Such a question would be valid only if it were a matter of some separate deed, of some simple happening among other happenings to be remembered or forgotten. But, as has already been pointed out, this is not so. We are imbued with the memory of a lost paradise, we do in fact possess an awareness of some disunity at the very ground of our life—no mere sense of individual transgression, but a deep-rooted tendency issuing from some primal experience of the human consciousness. Whenever and wherever man is aware of these things, there he believes in, or at least has an insight into, the mystery of original sin, even though he may not attach much meaning to the historical account of the paradisial happenings. Such awareness gives him eyes for the realities of life and of human nature; it guards him from illusions about himself and about others and intensifies his sense of responsibility towards himself and towards others. And, finally (provided it does not degenerate into morbid inferiority complex or Schopenhauerian self-pity), such awareness points to man's need of the transcendent act of divine redemption and forgiveness if he is to fulfil his destiny.

Chapter II

PROVIDENCE

(a) Greek Ideas

The thought of God watching over the life of the world, directing the course of History, judging its actions and bringing it ultimately back to unity with Himself, is a thought without which one can hardly think of God at all. This is what Christians mean by 'providence'. But providence, whether as 'moral government' which is said to concern the welfare and destiny of man, or as God's 'preservation' in respect of all events and the way in which a divine purpose is accomplished in and through them, is not an exclusively Judeo-Christian conception. The conviction that the world is not self-sufficient or that the world's relation to God is not confined to its being merely brought into existence and then left to its own resources; the conviction also that everything in the world and in the destinies of men is ordained according to the wisdom of some supreme and living pattern or power—are already present in early Greek philosophy. They have acquired a highly articulate form in the thought of Aristotle, who replaced the teleological myths of Platonism by a philosophy of motion issuing in the concept of a 'first mover' (πρῶτον κινοῦν) which, though itself without movement or change, communicates its energy or form to the world of change and sets the world in motion. The Aristotelian deity, however, is an entirely abstract concept involving an extraneous view of the relation of God and the world, which is, curiously enough, coupled with a tendency to monism. Though God, according to Aristotle, is the moving power which determines the life of Nature, he remains wholly unaffected by this life: he is wrapped in solitary contemplation of himself and does not enter in any real relation with the world, apparently unconscious of the very existence of anything but himself. There is thus nothing specifically 'religious' in Aristotle's teleology: it may perhaps relieve our minds of the awkward necessity of thinking of God as beholding and tolerating all the

evils of the world, but at the same time it leaves us shut up within the crushing reality of all our perplexities.

A more deeply religious providentialism is characteristic of various types of Stoicism. 'Est Deus in nobis. Agitante calescimus illo. Impetus hic sacrae semina, mentis habet.' Godhead here is the principle of life penetrating into and manifesting itself in the plenitude of all things: it is the prime force determining life in its being and becoming, the creative and directive reason ($\lambda\acute{o}\gamma os$) and the governing providence ($\pi\rho\acute{o}\nu o\iota a$). As, however, God and the world are identified and may be distinguished only 'in theory', providence acquires the character of a compelling force, of an inflexible necessity ($\grave{a}\nu\acute{a}\gamma\kappa\eta$) or inexorable fate ($\epsilon\acute{\iota}\mu a\rho\mu\acute{e}\nu\eta$).[1] Accordingly all things are produced in the stringent relentless succession of cause and effect, and all that happens to man is neither brought about nor conditioned by anything subjective to himself and could just as well have happened to anyone else. This identification of providence and fate is brought out very clearly in Seneca's treatise *De providentia*: fata nos ducunt, et quantum cuique restet, prima nascentium hora disposuit. Causa pendet ex causa, privata ac publica longus ordo rerum trahit. . . . Olium constitutum est, quid gaudeas, quid fleas (c.v.). It is well known how remorselessly the Stoics, and most particularly the Latin ones among them, demanded and applauded the subjection of all things and all men to a fixed universal law. This accounts to a large extent for their rather stuffy religiosity and their frequent indulgence in philistine considerations about the rationality, goodness and usefulness of all that happens and appears in the world-order (e.g. in Lactantius's *De ira Dei*)—an attitude that presented, undoubtedly, a reaction if compared with the grand Aristotelian conception of the immanent purposefulness of life.[2] But, inasmuch as it was imbued with an intense awareness of God's presence in the world, Stoicism had an important influence on Judeo-Christian conceptions, which are in some respects a synthesis of Hellenic and Hellenistic ideas with essential Jewish convictions. There is, however, one important and even decisive difference between these philosophies and biblical thought:

[1] $\epsilon\acute{\iota}\mu a\rho\mu\acute{e}\nu\eta$ is derived from $\mu\epsilon\acute{\iota}\rho o\mu a\iota$, to receive as one's portion, to have allotted to one, or, simply, to 'step into'—a very characteristic notion for the Classical attitude to life with its lack of feeling for personal freedom and the truly historical.

[2] See E. R. Bevan, *Stoics and Sceptics*.

their tendency to dissolve the living character of God and transform Him into an impersonal Absolute, standing in a relation of cause and effect to the world. They have converted divine purpose into a universally naturalistic category. It is not by chance that, as Collingwood observes,[1] the domain to which teleological metaphysics lies nearest and where it has asserted itself longest is that of organic nature, that is to say, in biology. Thus Aristotelian philosophy, a classic example of cosmic teleology, issues from a metaphysic of organic nature. This it extended to the whole of inorganic nature, to motion itself; and, in the end, all things are seen within one single teleological principle, in the pure energy of the 'first mover'. And, since teleological processes issue only from something capable of setting up and pursuing aims, this principle implies a rational activity. Accordingly, divine, absolute Reason determines everything. Providence here is an entirely unilateral, causal determination; and a naturalistic movement 'in space' is being substituted for historical dispensations. The modern equivalent of this substitution is the cult of the useful, which Darwin, in the name of his century, expressed in the biological terms of heredity, adaptation, natural selection, and all the other utility-causes denoting mechanical processes. The ideas of providence, destiny, 'synergism', and indeed of History itself, were thus finally supplanted by a mechanics in physiological garb.

(b) The Biblical Witness

Over against these latter philosophies stands the biblical revelation of God as intensely personal, the Creator and Sustainer of all that exists, the Father and the Judge of His creatures who goes out to seek and save, and the accompanying conception of man endowed with freedom and responsibility, fallen and yet redeemed and redeemable, sinful and hallowed.

The conception of divine providence in the Old Testament has undergone a long evolution, whose varied course cannot be pursued in the present context. The fact however is that one of the most fundamental, if not *the* fundamental, element of Jewish monotheism, as evidenced particularly by the prophets, is its belief in God's providence and God's guidance in History. Jahve is the living God who acts in History and exercises his

[1] See R. G. Collingwood, *The Idea of Nature.*

99

power in the issue of events. History itself is conceived as the story of divine acts wherein God gives meaning to the destiny of His chosen people, and through them to that of mankind as a whole. God is represented as choosing, and making covenant with, a selected group to be the agents of His universal purpose, as is declared in the call of Abraham: 'In thy seed shall all the families of the earth be blessed.' God's purpose acts 'concentrically', and Israel's destiny becomes the way in and through which this purpose is to take universal effect. Hence the characteristically Jewish ideas of *fulfilment* and *messianism*. The Jewish consciousness lives for ever by *amor futuri*: it lives in an intense expectation of some decisive event in the history of Israel, and of mankind as a whole, which will bring with it a solution of the perplexities of human existence. Thus it is that the Jewish consciousness is historical *par excellence*: a witness to the End as alive in the present and pressing on towards ultimate consummation. God becomes an historical reality through the existence of the Jews.

But the purposive acts of God in the world are not unilateral: he submits Himself to man's freedom; indeed He appears in History as one weak and apparently defeated: 'He delivers his strength into captivity and his glory into the enemies' hand' (Ps. lxxviii, 61). He appears as suffering in the sufferings of His chosen people, 'afflicted by their afflictions' (Isa. lxiii, 9) and appealing for their help (Isa. vi, 8). The 'anthropomorphism' of the Old Testament has been proverbially a stumbling block to many. But these anthropomorphic terms, though in a sense a projection of man's limited and imperfect mind on God, were themselves only possible because man is God's creature bearing the divine image within himself, and hence they denoted not a mere idea about God but the reality of God of which the human brain can frame no adequate idea at all. They are, in the words of Bishop Gore, not so much anthropomorphic language about God as theomorphic language about man. It is indeed preferable to run the risk of 'lowering' the conception of God sooner than think of Him as an abstraction or idea unrelated and extraneous to the world.

It is true that, because God is God, He must 'come into His own'—which is, in fact, an underlying motive of Old Testament providentialism. The universe is not a mere play of contingency: God 'has made a decree which shall not pass away' (Ps.

cxlviii, 6). He exercises a real power over and in all things that exist, leading them to their appointed End. And yet, paradoxical though this is and should be, this power is neither arbitrariness nor necessity, both of which reduce man to a marionette and paralyse his will. As a matter of fact, the reality of human freedom is even allowed to condition not only God's omnipotence but in some sense also His omniscience; and God is represented as waiting on man, entreating man, being disappointed in man. 'O my people, what have I done unto thee? and wherein have I wearied thee? testify against me' (Mic. vi, 3). There is, perhaps, no more powerful vindication of this fact than the drama of the book of Job, who challenged the divine justice and in that very challenge was approved by God; so also the struggle of Israel with the mysterious Unknown—a symbol of the whole destiny of the chosen people (Gen. xxxii, 24-30).

God's 'determination', then, is not mechanistic or causal but living and personal, involving reciprocity, that is to say, a relationship in which created beings and their pathways become real to God. His providence is not a system of laws or a mere drive of forces, immanent or transcendent: it presupposes a real and perfect personality as the ground of all existence, whose goodness is over all his works, by whom all things are sustained, and with whom men, as beings endowed with freedom, enter into equally real personal relationships. Such, in short, is the Old Testament view of providence.

The New Testament proclamation of the Father's holy and loving will towards all men and the whole creation and His lordship over 'heaven and earth' (Matt. xi, 25) stands in direct continuation with the Old Testament conceptions and, indeed, can only be understood if one appreciates the Jewish background against which it is adumbrated. But this will and lordship are no more conveyed in a mere message, nor shown in a general providential activity, but are revealed to man hypostatically, in person as well as in act. 'God so loved the world that he gave his only begotten Son . . . that the world through him might be saved.' And through His Son God leads the whole created universe, in its realms of Nature and History, to the ultimate fulfilment of the Kingdom of God which is to be a perfected fellowship of man with God and of man with man—a theme alike of the Old Testament and of the New. The evil and stricken pathways of 'this world' are followed by a perfect eternal order of

things through a 'regeneration' (παλιγγενεσία) of heaven and earth which is to overcome the opposition of the two orders in the eschatological fulfilment (Matt. xix, 28; Luke xx, 34-6). The creation, whose purpose is fulfilled in the Kingdom, is the domain of God's revelation, of His power and activity, by which all things are rendered significant and meaningful (Luke xii, 6-7). And even if we find that the element of tragedy in life is more manifest to us than that element of divine power and meaning which might reconcile us to it ('who will deliver me from the body of this death?'); even though we are faced with a situation in which God's providential illumination is locked in arduous struggle with 'darkness' (a dominant theme in the Apocalypse): yet we are given a promise that 'Wisdom is justified of her children' and 'rejoices' in the world. God as the sharer in the world's afflicted pathways is vindicated in its perplexing reality: in other words, God's very presence is also a victory in the world—a *Kingdom*. 'All power is given unto me in heaven and on earth' (Matt. xxviii, 18).

But the Gospels, just as the Old Testament, proclaim that no accomplishment of God's purposes is possible without our participating in it, without God Himself seeking our cimplicity in the victory of life. 'From the days of John the Baptist until now the Kingdom of God suffereth *violence* (βιάζεται), and the violent *take it by storm*' (ἁρπάζουσιν αὐτήν) (Matt. xi, 12). And more than this: 'He that believeth on me, the works that I do shall he do also; and greater works than these shall he do' (John xiv, 12).

The subsequent witness of the apostolic and post-apostolic times expresses the same truths in a different and sometimes more systematic language. This applies above all to St. Paul. His providentialism receives its most powerful expression in the Epistle to the Romans. The state of those who believe is seen here as a link in the chain of divine acts of grace which go back to God's eternal salvatory counsel and reach out to the eternal goal of God's Kingdom, in which the creature 'shall be delivered from the bondage of corruption into the glorious liberty of the sons of God'. History is shown as the story of the operation of God's purpose to redeem and save fallen mankind in Jesus Christ and to make it the body of the risen Lord—a new humanity and people of God. In the certainty of this faith St. Paul does not feel the need of entering into a theoretical consideration of

all sorts of intellectual difficulties, which seldom arise for those
who are really aware of the reality involved. Thus it seems to
him perfectly self-evident that God's saving activity and man's
freedom and responsibility co-inhere, however much such co-
inherence may offend the canons of logical consistency: on the
one hand 'God hath mercy on whom he will have mercy, and
(even more arbitrarily) whom he will he hardeneth' (Rom
ix, 18); on the other, we are 'labourers together with God'
(1 Cor. iii, 9) and are 'to work out our own salvation' (Phil.
ii, 12).[1]

What is true of 'the few elect', of 'the faithful remnant' underlies St. Paul's interpretation of History as a whole, however
far-reaching the destructive forces of human sin, since God's
saving purpose as revealed in Christ is not something apart from
or side by side with other things: it is the Beginning and the
End. God's eternal counsel to establish his Kingdom and his
promise to bring blessing and salvation to the whole human
race are irrevocable. And the whole creation strives for the
ultimate goal (Rom. viii, 18-22; 1 Cor. xv, 24-28), a goal, moreover, in which we share and by which we are activated, since
'we have the first-fruits of the Spirit' (Rom. viii, 23).

But what is perhaps the deepest insight into the nature of
God's providence is shown by St. Paul in chapters ix-xi of the
same Epistle, the main theme of which is an interpretation of
the destiny of Israel. How are we to comprehend the mysterious
fact that Israel, the chosen people of the ancient dispensation to
whom all the promises belong, finds itself alienated from the fulfilment of these promises, while the pagan world appears as
their actual bearer?[2] 'Have they stumbled that they should fall?
God forbid: but rather through their fall salvation is come to
the Gentiles': 'That blindness in part is happened to Israel, until
the fulness of the Gentiles be come in. And so Israel shall be
saved'; 'For the gifts and callings of God are without repentance' (Rom. xi, 11-31; cf. 2 Cor. iii, 14-16). The tragic destiny
of Israel not only allows but calls for its opposite: its very
alienation restores to it new value. Israel's strickenness, its sufferings, its questionings, are their own answer, and the judgment of God and of History on the chosen people is, in a sense,

[1] See also Rom. xv, 17; 1 Cor. vi, 20; vi, 9–11; Gal. v, 19–23.
[2] Cf. Hos. ii, 23: 'I will say to them which were not my people, Thou art
my people; and they shall say, Thou art my God.'

a judgment for it. Israel is the Cross on which the Saviour of the world is nailed, and through her sacrificial rejection of Christ salvation is come to the whole world.

This means, if we apply St. Paul's interpretation to the general problem of divine providence, that God is made known as Creator, Sustainer and Redeemer even in the most profligate and terrible ways and acts of men—in the world as it is given to us and not in an unreal world of dreamlike perfections. It is such a vision of God's mysterious pathways that makes St. Paul proclaim: 'All things work together for good to them that love God, to them who are called according to his purpose' (Rom. vii, 28). In this sense the whole realm of Nature and History should be regarded as the Kingdom of God, in spite of —or should one say because of?—the veil which now covers their glory.

If to St. Paul the providential order was still to some extent a veiling rather than a revealing of God's presence in the world, to St. John the Incarnation manifested once for all and unmistakably the whole meaning and End of History, which meaning and End are fulfilled and interpreted by the Holy Spirit. Accordingly Jesus Christ is not the crowning keystone in the arch of evolving humanity, not a super-natural miracle that may or may not be authentic, but God who becomes flesh; and as such he is to be understood as 'the way, the truth, and the life', the Light 'which lighteth every man that cometh into the world', *Alpha* and *Omega*, the Beginning and the End.

In both St. Paul and St. John, however, the great turning point in God's dealings with man and man's own destiny is the fact of the incarnate, crucified, risen and ascended Lord followed by the gift of the Spirit or the coming of the Paraclete— He who enables the world to be in Christ and Christ in it.

(c) *The Patristic Witness*

The theology of the Apologists which, despite its various shortcomings, represents an important attempt to depict Christianity as the only true, because revealed, philosophy displays its peculiarities most distinctly in its doctrine of providence. It stands, above all, in conscious opposition to pagan polytheism, to the dualism of the Gnostics and Manicheans, and to the fatalism of the Stoics and Epicureans. It is highly misleading

to describe the Apologists, or, for the matter of that, the subsequent patristic literature, as '*akute Hellenisierung des Christentums*' (Harnack) in which Hellenism is alleged to have triumphed over Judaism which was inherited by Christianity. In point of fact it was an *akute Christianisierung des Hellenismus*; and though certain motives of Greek theism were accepted (which was inevitable in the great encounter between the Church and the world, to which the Church was driven to explain itself); though it was recognized that God had not left Himself without witnesses among the Gentiles, the power or *dynamis* of these motives was seen to be that of the Gospel. They were, indeed, fundamentally modified and sometimes even deliberately distorted so as to render the terminology of ancient thought expressive of a new and basically biblical experience. 'It has not pleased God to give his people salvation in dialectic' (Ambrose); and Tertullian exclaimed 'credibile est quia ineptum est! Certum est quia impossibile!'

The Apologists, then, leave us in no doubt about the biblical basis of their theism. Their faith is the faith in God, the Creator of the world, the Father of all and Sustainer of the course of events, who through his Church guides the destinies of mankind; their hope is the hope in Resurrection (Athenagoras, Theophilus of Antioch, Irenaeus). But their providentialism is characterized by an intense cosmological concern, which is most evident in their attempt to express specifically biblical ideas through the Stoic doctrine of the all-pervading divine logos the influence of which is already seen in some Old Testament writers. The same tendency is characteristic of the Alexandrian school of theology. But, significantly enough, Clement of Alexandria rejects all rational proofs for ascertaining the reality of God's providence and all ready-made answers to the problem of theodicy (Strom. v, 1, 6). His own and his successors' (particularly Origen's) varied attempts to deal with the question of theodicy have this much in common, that, on the one hand, they strongly emphasize the fact of man's freedom and responsibility: this emphasis being largely due to the challenge of Gnostic fatalism, with its three fixed unalterable types of men (pneumatic, psychic, hylic). And, on the other hand, they banish all ideas of making God causally responsible for the evils of the present world-order. They declare, in accordance with the Platonic philosophical tradition, that evil has no essential char-

acter, no substance of its own, but is a bare negation and is real only in so far as it is borne by freedom and parasitically feeds on the good (cf. Origen, *Comm. in Ioan.* ii, 7; *De princ.* ii, 9, 2; Athanasius, *Contra gentes* vi and vii; Basil the Great, *Hexaemeron* ii, 4; Gregory of Nyssa, *Oratio catech.* vi; and others).

The concept which epitomizes almost all patristic doctrines of providence is that of 'economy' (οἰκονομία), a term which originally had the very pedestrian connotation of administering or supervising an office.[1] But administration implies method, and thus 'economy' acquired the meaning of plan and design. 'God', says the *Epistle of Diognetus* (ix, 1) quoted by Prestige, 'had already "economized" with himself together with his Son, the things prepared from the beginning.' Providence in this sense implies the eternal counsels of God; but it also concerns the gifts that God sends and supplies in a providential manner and his 'designs' and 'dispositions' as exhibited in the events of History.[2] In Origen's opinion God 'economizes' whole cyclic ages or aeons (which he, together with some of the Fathers, regarded as a name for defined periods of Time).

Origen used another term, which derived from St. Paul's theology and reappears in the writings of the orthodox Fathers, viz. *mysterion*: it expresses the Christological aspect of divine providence and of human and cosmic History and denotes the relation of Christ to the world in His redeeming and sanctifying power. God has 'made known unto us the mystery of His will according to his good pleasure which he hath purposed in himself: that in the dispensation of the fulness of times he might gather together in one all things in Christ, both which are in heaven, and which are on earth' (Eph. i, 9-10). Indeed, all divine providence is seen by the Fathers as centred in and issuing from the fact of the incarnate Lord, for which the words *oikonomia* is the classic term from the third century onward.[3] It is here that patristic thought exhibits its profound insight into the ways of the self-revelation of God in History and the

---

[1] See G. L. Prestige, *God in Patristic Thought*, ch. iii.

[2] Op. cit. p. 59.

[3] This did not preclude their recognition of the presence and operation of other spiritual forces, good and evil, angels and demons, which, in accordance with the biblical conviction, were seen to share constantly and actively in the life of the world and of men. See S. Bulgakov's *The Ladder of Jacob*—probably the most important work among the many attempts at Christian angelology.

ensuing dynamism of the historical process. History is the sphere of God's kenotic 'accommodation' (John Chrysostom) or 'consideration' (Gregory Naz.), of God's 'acquiescence' or 'concession' (Maximus Conf.). 'God loves us not as we are, but as we are becoming' (Augustine); 'God renders himself accordant with our ways' (Irenaeus). When God's word is spoken and revealed in History, it is not an immutable, timeless, static proposition which ignores the concreteness of historic situations and the differences between past and future, but a timeful activity in which creation is going on all the time; an activity which some Fathers designate by the word 'revolution' (cf. Gregory Naz. *Oratio* xxxi). Thus it is that St. John Chrysostom could boldly declare in an explanation of the 'relative' character of the Old Testament revelation: 'Do not ask how these (Old Testament precepts) can be good now when the need for them is past: ask how they were good when the period required them. Or rather, if you wish, do inquire into their merit even now, it is still conspicuous, and lies in nothing so much as what now enables us to find fault with them. Their highest praise is that we now see them to be defective. . . . And how can the same thing be good at one time and bad at another? I ask rather, how should it not be so, when we have regard to the plain teaching of the fact of growth in all things. . . . Consider the facts of History. All agree that murder is an invention of Satan, yet this very act at a suitable time made Phineas to be honoured with the high priesthood. Phineas's murder 'was reckoned to him for righteousness'. Just in the same way Abraham obtained an even higher honour for being not a murderer only but what was much worse, a child-murderer. We must not then look at the facts in themselves only, but investigate with attention the period also, the origin, the motive, the difference of persons, and all the attendant circumstances: so only can one get at the truth' (*On St. Matt.* xvii, 5-6).

(d) Western Writers

It is now necessary to consider some speculative aspects of the problem of divine providence which have received the attention of many Christian writers, particularly in the West.

If we discard the doctrines of deism, which treats God as a kind of absentee deity and refuses to recognize his indwelling

power (a position which, it may be noted in parenthesis, is a very easy target for criticism, seeing that it must needs issue in a conception of the universe devoid of life, of meaning, of volition, perhaps even of hostility: in short, as Carlyle remarked, one huge lifeless, immeasurable steam-engine, rolling on, in its dead indifference, 'to grind me limb from limb'): if, then, we discard these deistic abstractions, how are we to conceive of the relations between God and man? This question was first fully considered by St. Augustine in his discussion of the problem of divine grace and human freedom (or, rather, lack of human freedom) and, as we have already seen, he was led to construe the precarious doctrine of ethical necessitarianism and of double predestination. On the basis of this fundamental doctrine and of the ensuing conception of providence he formulated in his *De civitate Dei* a monumental philosophy of History which anticipates the coming of an era of secular History controlled by Satan with occasional interventions of God urging men to escape the shattered prison-house of the City of this world.[1]

It fell to Boethius, over a century later, to contribute substantially to the discussion of the problem of divine-human relations, and in particular of God's providence. His contribution, far removed from the old and sterile Stoic tolerance of things as indifferent, even though he himself was influenced by Stoicism, was a real spark of fire in what appeared to be a purely theoretical discussion. In his famous dialogue *De consolatione philosophiae*, which has been called the most widely read book in the Middle Ages, Boethius makes an important attempt at reconciling God's fore-knowledge with man's free will. I shall not enter into a discussion of his treatment of this intricate problem. His greatest contribution lay probably in the fact of his intense awareness of the problem.[2] And whatever be thought of his endeavours he has fully acknowledged the reality of human freedom and succeeded in avoiding the pitfalls of determinism,

---

[1] It is, however, significant that almost the entire political development of the Middle Ages was dominated by this treatise, and was in a sense responsible for the creation of the Holy Roman Empire. Augustinism may have saved the Western Church from idolizing the State, but it has done so at a great price—at the price of the ascendency of the worldly claims of papal power, of clericalism and papal self-idolization.

[2] 'What heavenly power', asks Boethius, 'has set such a strife between two truths (divine fore-knowledge and human freedom)? Thus, though, apart, each brings no doubt, they cannot be linked together' (v. 3).

Providence

which is all the more remarkable in view of his Stoic affiliations.[1]

We must now turn once more to St. Thomas Aquinas who did much to clarify the question of the relation between God and the world. The position of St. Thomas is to a large extent Augustinian; but, while Augustine's interest was predominantly soteriological, his was metaphysical *par excellence* and as such more Aristotelian than Augustinian. In spite of all the complexities and attenuations introduced by Aquinas (which make a precise assessment of his majestic edifice very difficult and which have, in fact, led many Thomists to almost contradictory conclusions) his providentialism, as has already been noted above, does not seem to have avoided the quicksands of determinism.

Aquinas's treatment of the problem starts from the Aristotelian conception of God as the 'first cause' and from the ensuing contention that no being or mode of being can escape divine causality; and it is assumed that unless this is accepted God is reduced to a dependant, if not a puppet, of the creature. *Dieu déterminant ou déterminé, pas de milieu!* (Garrigou-Lagrange).[2] From this idea of God as the primal cause and mover it is concluded that every act and every movement of the creatures must emanate (*emanatio*) from the first cause. But God moves necessary and free agents to free activity, thus, it is argued, rendering the will *in actu primo* capable of freely determining itself *in actu secundo*. This includes sin, except that God is the originator only of the 'physical entity' of sin, not of its 'formal malice'. Inasmuch as the divine influence precedes in order of causality all acts of the free creature, the motion emanating from God takes on the character of a 'physical premotion' (*praemotio physica*) or 'physical predetermination' (*prae-*

---

[1] Boethius also saw the close connection between the definition of Eternity and the problem of divine fore-knowledge, and he corrected the simple Time-reference in the notions of predestination and fore-knowledge which seems to have misled many theologians. He rightly attacks the idea of God knowing things before they happen; and he maintains that for God, who is 'the eternal present', they have already happened (which is rather controversial). Hence his famous definition of Time as the *Nunc* which 'imitates' the eternal present of God. This conception was taken over by Aquinas: 'eternitas est interminabilis vitae tota simul et perfecta possessio'. See F. H. Brabant, op. cit., lect. iii.

[2] For texts see *Summa theol.* i. quaestiones 10, 14, 19, 22–23, 83, 103–105; *Contra Gent.* ii. 91; De Potentia iii. 7; De Malo ix. 6. See also Sergius Bulgakov, *The Bride of the Lamb*; Hermann Schell, *Katholische Dogmatik*; Garrigou-Lagrange, *Dieu, son Existence et sa Nature*, and d'Alès, *Providence et Libre Arbitre*.

determinatio physica) of the free acts, and the free will infallibly consents to that to which it is premoved, for the premotion is always 'efficacious'. True, the will has the power to dissent, but it dissents (or consents) according to that to which it is premoved; in other words, physical premotion determines the act regardless of the fact whether the human will can resist or not.

Now if these philosophical principles are carried from the domain of 'nature' to that of 'super-nature' or grace, grace (*gratia efficax*) must be regarded as a physical premotion of the will to the performance of a good act. The will thus predetermined corresponds with a metaphysical necessity to grace. It remains a secret (a secret rather than a mystery, for it is Thomism itself that began to rationalize the mystery of divine-human relations and should now look squarely and unevasively into the difficulties it has brought about): it remains a secret how this necessity, which is called *necessitas consequentiae*, or for that matter the general premoving metaphysical necessity, can subsist simultaneously with freedom. It appears that grace is efficacious not on the grounds that its operation is intrinsically a free relationship, but because it predetermines the will to consent.[1] Thus it is that the relentless and logical sequence of the idea of *prima causa* and *primus motor* is carried through all the aspects of divine-human relations; and these relations turn out to be not, strictly speaking, relations between God and man, since, as St. Thomas says, 'every relation which we consider between God and the creature is really in the creature by whose change the relation is brought about, whereas it is not in God, but only in our way of thinking'.[2]

The notion of premotion or predetermination underlies also the Thomist approach to the question of divine knowledge, for in this premotion is found the medium by which God's omniscience infallibly foresees all future acts, whether absolute or conditional, of his creatures. Divine knowledge itself is divided according to the diversity of objects, in particular, into 'know-

---

[1] As to *gratia sufficiens*, which imparts only the *posse*, not the *agere*, this is in reality a gratia insufficiens, about which some have prayed: 'a gratia sufficiente libera nos Domine!'

[2] In the Christological context this means that, strictly speaking, even in Christ there can be no real assumption of manhood by God nor any self-limitation of the divine nature in the human. That is what, in fact, St. Thomas declares: 'the union of the two natures in Christ is not really in God, except only in our way of thinking; but in the human nature, which is a creature, it is real' (*S. th.* iii, qu. 2. 7).

ledge of vision' (*scientia visionis*), which refers to things that have existed, exist or will exist, and a (hypothetical) 'knowledge of simple understanding' (*scientia simplicis intelligentiae*), which is said to refer to the purely possible, that is to say, to things that have not existed, do not exist and, presumably, will not exist. If this is so, it is argued, God must know a future act by the knowledge of vision; and this knowledge necessarily implies a divine decree. Hence no future free act can exist unless God decrees its existence.

As is well known, this and the whole problem of the relation of God and human freedom was a matter of bitter controversy, which centred round Bañez and the Jesuit Molina and has been going on ever since.[3] The importance of Molinism in this controversy, however, was mainly negative: it has shown—in the opinion of many irrefutably—that the Thomist position is subversive of human freedom and must needs result in determinism. But it was unable to challenge Thomism on more positive grounds, since it started from the same or similar premises, treating freedom as a special kind of causality side by side with, or subordinate to, the prime causality of God and attempting to adjust the two. Molina's concern in his *Concordia liberi arbitrii cum gratiae donis* was to find a medium whereby God knows a future free act independently of the divine decree. This medium he finds in that kind of divine knowledge which refers neither to the purely possible nor yet to the actually existing but to those events or things which would exist if certain conditions were realized. Such events are called conditioned future events or *futurabilia*. Now God knows these by the *scientia media*, which is midway, as it were, between 'knowledge of vision' and 'knowledge of simple understanding' and by which divine providence in the world is said to be safeguarded. Thus God knows with certainty what man will do by his own innate liberty if he be placed in such or such circumstances to which alone the divine

---

[3] See de Régnon, *Bañez et Molina*. Histoire, Doctrines, Critique Metaphysique. . . . It is interesting and paradoxical that in the sphere of sociology Thomism and Molinistic Jesuitism represent exactly the opposite tendencies to those of their respective metaphysics: while Jesuitism is proverbially authoritarian or even 'totalitarian' and tends to disfranchise man, Thomism, on the contrary, exhibits a much freer, more organic and, to use a modern term, personalistic idea of society based on a genuine 'Christian humanism'. It is this perhaps: the articulation and defence of Christian humanism which constitutes St. Thomas's most enduring contribution to Christian thought.

decree applies. The certitude of divine knowledge is due therefore not to the intrinsic efficacy of the decree, but to the *scientia media* which without prejudice to the free will sees the consent before the decree.

It must be noted that the whole notion of *scientia media* is exceedingly involved and, altogether, seems to substitute one difficulty for another. The really important contribution of the Molinists, in so far as it is possible to detect a unanimity among them, is to have shown that God does not know the future free acts in any absolute, actual decree of his will and that the certain knowledge of an effect in its cause, as conceived by Aquinas, must needs be the knowledge of a necessary effect and thus amounts to a denial of human freedom.[1]

The whole *praemotio-physica*-argument, which underlies the Thomist teaching on providence, must indeed be regarded as deterministic, as undermining the active and creative spontaneity of the creature's freedom, even though this determinism appears to have its limit in the assumption of a kind of restricted choice on the part of man. There is, ontologically speaking, no room for freedom, it being a mere 'secondary' cause which does not originate anything and does not even in any real sense co-operate with, but only receives and transmits, the energy of the 'first' cause. If, to use a metaphor cited by Bulgakov in his criticism of the doctrine of predestination, Mount Everest were to descend with all its weight on a thin nail stuck into soft wood, it is humbug to talk about this nail's capacity of choice or free determination, of going or not going into the wood. Such choice or free determination is simply annulled by the pressure of the mountain. There is in fact no option in the face of divine premotion. Molina was perfectly right when he said, with reference to sin, that since the divine influence, which premoves *ad unum*, both introduces sin as an act and entity and simultaneously withholds the opposite premotion to a good act, sin becomes an inescapable fatality. So does the whole of human existence in its tragedy and promise, and God's providence, instead of being a communion and dialogue between God and

[1] The Jesuit Erich Przywara writes: 'Molina's *scientia media* besagt, dass das Individuum nicht einfachhin Schnittpunkt von Allgemeingesetzen sei und darum von Gott in der Bestimmung dieser Allgemeingesetze erkannt werde, sondern unmittelbar in sich vor den Augen Gottes stehe und darum Voraussetzung, nicht rein Folge der goettlichen Vorsehung sei' (*Religionsphilosophie der Katholischen Theologie*, Die Geschichtlichen Richtungen, 1).

his creature, turns out to be a kind of divine comedy in which the almighty and omniscient God is confronted with himself in eternal, untold self-gratification.

(e) Causality

Our contention, then, is that an interpretation of the relations of God and the world in terms of causality, in the sense of a divine causation which determines all things throughout and of 'secondary' causes, such as human freedom or even the forces we see in Nature are supposed to be, results in necessitarianism with the implied unreality of 'secondary causes'. The world acquires the character of a mere projection of the first cause, and if there remains any room at all for the existence of the world this is only possible at the price of what to all intents and purposes amounts to monism, in which all creatures, whether free or not, are seen as imprisoned in the iron framework of an all-pervading divine causality.

As a matter of fact, no type of causality, efficient, final or otherwise, can avoid a picture of the world where all things, and the world itself, are merely pushed or pulled into life, and where the end is a ready-made datum, while the process leading to that end runs on predetermined lines. All creativity and spontaneity on the part of the world and of man are therefore lost. Above all, this picture eliminates the image alike of the living hypostatic God, sharing in the life of his creation, and of man, endowed with freedom and creatively fulfilling the call of his destiny. In forcing the rigid scheme of causal connections upon their relations it attempts to deal with the mystery of divine-human life mechanically and relying on the weapons of naturalistic abstractions.

We shall offer no apology for insisting again and again on this radical opposition between causal connections (in whatever garb) and relations pertaining to divine and human life, even though this may appear to be in some measure a verbal or terminological opposition. But we here reach a point where language shows its profoundly symbolical meaning, and where differences of speech become differences of meaning, of feeling for and attitude to life. It may be true that the word 'cause' has a different connotation for Aristotle and the Scholastics, to whom anything goes by the name 'cause' which in any of the

various senses of that word provides an answer to the question of *Why*, while, e.g. in the metaphysics of Hume and, generally speaking, since the eighteenth century, it began to denote something strictly antecedent to, and mechanically connected with another something called the effect. It may be true that none of the various kinds of causes as manipulated by Aristotle or Thomas Aquinas involves 'an infinite successive process of which the first cause is itself a member, except that it happens to have no predecessor'.[1] Nevertheless in both cases the language of causality shows a consciousness which conceives of reality as copied from a world-picture drawn by physics, or at any rate from a naturalistic world pervaded by externality, in which everything is extraneous to everything else, and, instead of revealing, rationalizes and distorts the mystery of divine-human relations. The travesties of causal language when applied to the relations between God and man are particularly evident in their unbiblical preclusion of any mutuality of these relations. So long, however, as the 'cause' is looked upon as what by its action exclusively determines the nature of the 'effect' in a passive object, life is impossible as well as inconceivable. In the realm of life and personal relations, as distinct from that of purely mechanical processes, an action cannot be conceived which is out of relation to that upon which it acts, and any change attributed to God as 'cause' must be related to, and in so far determined by, the receiver of that action. God cannot be thought of as a kind of transcendent accumulator charged with a constant original energy, which may be released from time to time. The least we are compelled to say is that it depends on the nature of the receiver how he will behave under God's action. In other words the action must be reciprocal. But such reciprocity is explicitly repudiated by St. Thomas.

Furthermore, causal metaphysics is in the end incapable of facing the specifically historical problem of divine providence and of human destiny. As Spengler and other historicists have pointed out, causality as such gives answers only concerning the fact *that* something happens, to the questions of *Why* or *How*, that is to say, to the problems belonging to the order of the things of Nature; but it does not and cannot answer the question of *When*. And as the web of cause and effect spreads over our

---

[1] Cf. the discussion of this question by Eric Mascall, one of the most outstanding Thomists in the Church of England, in his *He Who Is*, ch. v.

vision of life there is formed a picture of timeless processes, expressing all that is thing, property, law, datum, perhaps even happening or incident, but suppressing all that is Providence, History, Event, Destiny. Indeed these latter realities form a world of their own—they pertain to the mystery of God-manhood, from which the world of causes and effects is as widely removed as possible.

The Christian champions of traditional aitiological metaphysics usually reply to these criticisms by referring to the facts of revelation which, they assert, 'supplement' their avowedly defective philosophy. But such supplementation is only conceivable if there is consistency and intrinsic relation between the two. No such relation, however, can possibly be construed between the concepts of first cause, of physical premotion and physical predetermination, on the one hand, and the ideas of God's self-revelation in creation, providence and redemption, of his self-disclosure in History and his living personal communion with his free creatures, on the other. And when we are told that it is possible 'in theory' to divorce the 'supernatural' from the 'natural' and that, in the words of Dom Chapman, 'scholastic philosophy deals *only* with the natural, and therefore not with life in all its complexity as we know it, but with the world as it would be without revelation and without grace (of all kinds), which are disturbing factors',[1] we can only conclude that such a philosophy is irrelevant: revelation and grace must indeed be very 'disturbing' factors for it![2] In point of fact, revelation is *not* a supplementation—a notion that could be applied to the world of extraneous things and objects only—but the End, in the sense in which we have tried to define this term above, to be more precise, the Beginning and the End, *Alpha* and *Omega*. 'I am the way, the truth, and the life.' In other words, if revelation is an event in the very depth of being, as indeed it is pre-eminently, it must be affirmed to be as intensely relevant at the initial stage of our knowledge of God and the

[1] See the description of the relation between 'natural' and 'revealed' theology in his *Spiritual Letters*, quoted by Mascall, op. cit.

[2] One is reminded here of the words of a saintly Roman Catholic theologian in Germany who said that 'the Aristotelian-Thomistic philosophy is the millstone which will drag Catholicism over the precipice if Catholicism does not get rid of it' (die Aristotelisch-Thomistische Philosophie ist der Muelstein, der den Katholizismus in den Abgrund ziehen wird, wenn er nicht von ihm befreit wird) (quoted in the somewhat Quixotic and unruly but almost pathetically honest *Der Katholizismus, sein Stirb und Werde*).

ultimate meaning of existence as at its final stage. Indeed, only return to these ultimate depths renders philosophical thinking a possibility at all. This is true for a materialist as much as for a Christian, even though the materialist may conceive of God as matter, for the materialist's question is as much a witness to the living God as any other true question. The two ends of the chain of human thought must, therefore, be integrated into a single existential act of knowledge.

Chapter III

GOD-MANHOOD

We must now turn to a constructive discussion of the various problems concerning divine providence. We shall set out by re-stating that God is not the cause but the Creator of the world—a fact which is of course recognized by the scholastics as much as by anybody else; but they tend to invalidate this fact by substituting Aristotelianism for the decisive testimony of revelation, and thus make this recognition inconsistent with their philosophical conception of God. God reveals Himself, His own life, His own 'energy' *ad extram*, in the void 'in which' He creates the world. But this creative self-revelation of God is not merely an eternal changeless activity of perfection which becomes the cause of action in his creature: the created beings acquire an immanent force of their own; they become, in a sense, self-existent, and God enters into a positive relation with them, continues to act in them within this relationship and, in calling man to co-operate in its realization, fulfils his purpose towards them. In other words, the world is not merely drawn onwards by something outside itself but is possessed 'from the beginning' of an intrinsic activity of its own, which creates all the various types of being found in the world and which is born, according to the witness of the Book of Genesis, of the primeval Earth, of the meonic darkness of dawning life.

Nature may appear to us in a lifeless continuity, but she hides within her the violence and suddenness of creative growth and action: she is not an order of immutable cosmic hierarchies but rather a cosmogonic process. This seems to be confirmed by modern physics, which proclaims that at the very basis of Nature an element of indeterminism is to be found.[1] It differs,

[1] I do not pretend to understand the scientific aspect of this view, which is in fact entirely beyond me. Eddington in his *The Nature of the Physical World* clearly acknowledges such indeterminism, in apparent conflict with the old-fashioned idea of 'the universal reign of laws', which are, in the last analysis, but formulated descriptions of certain kinds of behaviour under

however, fundamentally from Aristotle's idea of a world of self-moving things, since for Aristotle the various forms of change in Nature represent an eternal uniform rotation, and the objects of change are related among themselves not temporally but logically: that is to say, movement here is in no way related to History.

The indeterminate nature of the created universe may appear as chaos, as the seething unleashed potentiality of elemental darkness, as sheer force, whose only inherent characteristic is to flow, to push infinitely onwards. Chaos may terrify us: but it is from Cosmos rather than from Chaos that proceed all those evil necessities, impossibilities and limitations which transform our world into a vale of frustration. And yet Nature cannot be entirely aimless, with no guiding light outside her or any meaning within her (a conception characteristic of Bergson's evolutionism), since she cannot even exist out of relation to the One who is the ground of all creativity. She may and does glory in her own apparent regularity and self-sufficient order, but at the same time she reaches out to a yet unapparent meaning and thus fulfils a mysterious transcendent purpose.[2] This implies direction or orientation towards the realization of something not yet existent, and hence must needs be related to History.

But there is something in this world which, as we have seen, by force of its inherent nature has no efficient cause at all, namely the act of freedom. Man is a creature 'formed of the dust of the ground'; but God endowed him with His image and, in the significant words of Genesis, 'breathed into his nostrils the breath of life'—which signifies an effusion, a giving of God's own life or energy. That is why mankind is called 'the race of God'—*genos theou* (Acts xvii, 28–9): 'I have said; Ye are gods; and all of you are children of the most High' (Ps. lxxxii, 6).

more or less exact observation ('statistical averages'). This is why even science must be regarded as implying an act of faith, which, according to the classic definition in the Epistle to the Hebrews, is 'the substantiation of things hoped for and the assurance of things not seen'.

[2] This may even be regarded as a partial vindication of what Collingwood calls the Renaissance view of Nature, according to which, instead of being an 'organism', the natural world is an 'arrangement of bodily parts designed for a definite purpose by an intelligent mind beyond itself'. On this view, however, there can, in the last resort, be no real change at all, except for 'breaking down or wearing out'. In point of fact the world is not a finished product, or 'arrangement', or a finished system, but a creative process. See R. G. Collingwood, *The Idea of Nature*, Part ii, ch. 1.

God-manhood

Man is a living paradox of creatureliness and uncreatedness, of impotence and omnipotence: he is a slave and a lord, a creature and a creator. To state this paradox is evidently not a logical proposition, for logical propositions hate such contradictions like hell-fire itself. Of course, the concept of cause, of effect, of the unmoved and the moved are not self-contradictory. A cause is not an effect, and the unmoved is not the moved, just as a colonel is not a sergeant, and a professor not an undergraduate. The characteristics of these concepts are so definite as to present no problem if clearly stated. It is different if we try to master a reality not of our making: God and History, being and non-being, life and death, creatorship and createdness. In fact man lives by awareness of these paradoxes, and they are the hall-mark of his very nature. Such was, in particular, the conclusion at which we arrived in the discussion of the problem of human freedom. Man is a creature, and yet he is free throughout, imbued with a power of self-initiation. There is, we said, a human providence and a human fore-ordination. Imperfect, limited it may be and very far from the infinite providence of God, but nonetheless real, since human freedom and human creatorship are real. And these give man, a fallen and afflicted creature, the attributes of divinity. God steps down from his throne and dwells in the will of man. . . . Having come to these conclusions we are not bound to assert God's 'absoluteness' in the abstract and without qualification. Actually, we do make such qualifications —not because our concern is what God ought to be or how He ought to reveal himself, but because of what He is and how He has revealed Himself. The defect of Thomism (and in a different way of Augustinianism and Calvinism) lies in that it starts from a knowledge of God's absoluteness out of relation, extrinsic or intrinsic, to revelation, deduces logically from his eternal decrees, and so explains the destiny of man. We, on the contrary, start from revelation, which is the *terminus ad quem* and, for that very reason, the *terminus a quo* of our whole inquiry. Revelation, the *terminus ad quem*, we said, is an act in the very depth of being: it affects our whole thinking and modifies our conception of God's nature and attributes.[1]

---

[1] This has been very poignantly stated and discussed by Prof. Leonard Hodgson in *The Doctrine of the Trinity* (Introductory Lecture).
The fact that the Christian is called upon to speak to and to co-operate with a non-Christian world on grounds that are or are not common to them

The Beginning and the End

The qualifications, then, of God's absoluteness are that, having willed to create free beings, He has willed in this very act of creation and in the ensuing activity of His providence to submit Himself to a limitation, to a *kenosis* and a divesting of His power, to make, that is to say, human freedom the condition of these acts. 'He delivereth his strength into captivity and his glory into the enemies' hand.' Such self-delivery and self-limitation is, however, itself an act of freedom: it is an act of freedom in love and of love in freedom. God is not and cannot be limited by anything external to Him, for there are no things external to Him. This means that divine acts, to which supreme value adheres, are only made possible through the absence of absolute power on the part of what is regarded as the unconditional and absolute necessity of God. Paradoxical though it may be, precisely that which is a limitation in God's mode of existence, the inability or rather unwillingness to determine unilaterally the creature in its being and becoming, is a fact of infinite value and reveals the true nature of God. It is so, even though this very fact is set over against that absolute perfection and 'necessity' of God without which we do not seem to be able to think of God at all. The relation of the two facts, however, that is, of God's absolute claim over His creature and of His *kenosis*, with the ensuing reality of the creature's freedom—their reciprocal balance and self-limitation—is itself a supreme value. In this relation is revealed the mystery of God-manhood, to which we have already referred on several occasions and which we shall now endeavour to discuss more fully.

(a) *The God-Man*

The term 'God-manhood', or rather its adjective form 'divine-human', though not of strictly scriptural origin, was first formulated in patristic Christology with the explicit aim of bring-

---

is based not on his ability to abstract himself provisionally and, so to say, with an *arrière-pensée* from revelation, always ready to patch the old garment with pieces from the new, but on the fact that the God of revelation is indivisible Wholeness, the Creator and Sustainer, the Beginning and the End of all things visible and invisible; on the fact that the Son of God is God made man who goes to the last confines of the pathways of human existence. We ourselves as Christians are, therefore, engaged in the limitations and contradictions of a fallen and God-denying humanity, and experience to the utmost the forces of death that inclose it: we are never more Christian than when we identify ourselves with the rest of mankind.

ing out the fundamental unity of Christ's person.[1] It is not our task to pursue the development of Christological dogma or to show in detail how this formulation came about. It will be sufficient to mention that at the culminating point of this development, at the Council of Chalcedon (451), a formula was found which expressed the fact that Christ is in all his manifestations one and the same person, or *hypostasis*, who nevertheless subsists in two distinct natures, or *physeis*, divine and human. The formula raised however considerable difficulties, of which the Fathers were fully aware, and which emerged nowhere more clearly than in the subsequent as well as in the preceding Christological controversies. One of the main difficulties which was authoritatively dealt with at the sixth oecumenical council concerned the question as to the presence of two wills and consciousnesses in Christ. Since 'nature' includes the will and consciousness, it was asked, are we not postulating a dualism, that is, the conception of two wills and two consciousnesses lying *side by side* in the same person, with the result that the life of Christ is seen as a constant alternation between His manhood and His Godhead, a conception against which Cyril of Alexandria had fought so ardently in his time? It was in the context of this and such like questions that Cyril, Gregory of Nyssa and the Areopagite had taught the doctrine of one energy in Christ, the latter with the definite addition *theandrike*, divine-human.

Dionysius's argument is summed up in the following question: How can Jesus, *o panton epekeina*, be essentially united with all men, that is, not merely in the sense in which He who is the author of all men can be designated man—in accordance with the notion that God may be named with the names of His creatures—but in the sense that He was truly man as to His entire nature? Dionysius's answer is that He did not perform divine acts as God, nor human acts as man; but inasmuch as in Him God has become man, He developed a new, i.e. a divine-human, a theandric activity ($\theta\epsilon\alpha\nu\delta\rho\iota\kappa\grave{\eta}\nu$ $\grave{\epsilon}\nu\acute{\epsilon}\rho\gamma\epsilon\iota\alpha\nu$).[2] This argument was deepened and amplified by other dyotheletes, especially Maximus the Confessor and his disciple Anastasius, who taught that as the Logos conferred on man, created in his

[1] It has since become an inherent factor in the idiom of Russian Orthodox thought, though it has been used there somewhat indiscriminately.

[2] See *Ep.* 4 *ad Caium*, and the Commentary by Maximus the Confessor, ed. Halis, pp. 28–34.

image, the power of acting, as they put it, somato-psychically (ψυχανδρικῶς, σωματοψύχως), as a type of Christ; so did the Logos, in and in view of the Incarnation, act theandrically (θεανδρικῶς) in Christ. One may amplify this extremely important idea still more by saying that in the divine Word lies the eternal archetype of all created beings, and in particular of man, who is made in the image of God, so that the eternal Word is the archetypal or eternal Man who was always destined to act as the incarnate Lord (see John ii, 31 and 1 Cor. xv, 47). Recent Christologists have assigned the origin of this idea to Apollinarius of Laodicea (fourth century), but the doctrine of archetypal manhood can be found in the earliest patristic Christologies, particularly in connection with the Logos theology which treats of Christ as the image of God, and man as made in that image (cf. Athanasius), as well as in connection with Irenaeus's idea that in Christ the creation of man was completed and realized.[1] The same approach is characteristic of modern Orthodox

[1] Apollinarius, a profound Christian thinker, of whom Charles Raven says in his exhaustive study *Apollinarianism* that his theology was the source of all subsequent Christological thought, has yet paid for his undoubted awareness of the crux of the Christological problem by positing a unity between the human and the divine in Christ which involved a mutilation of the human. His heresy consists in that he realized and intended such a mutilation. Apollinarius's orthodox opponents, whatever their unfairness to him and blindness to his insights, were, nevertheless, right in rejecting his position on the grounds that 'what was not assumed was not redeemed'. They fought for a Christ who is not only truly divine but also perfectly human with all the faculties, spiritual as well as physical, proper to man, even though His manhood has no *separate* personality of its own. In other words they fought neither for an Apollinarian *theos sarkophoros* nor a Nestorian *anthropos theophoros*, but for the true *theanthropos*. Raven maintains that many orthodox Fathers were in fact Apollinarian but were too clever to acknowledge their master. This may be true to some extent, particularly in the case of Cyril of Alexandria, who brought back Apollinarius's doctrine 'by a deft concession in phraseology, a concession not greater than that which Athanasius had made to the Niceans' (op. cit.). It is even probable that some of Apollinarius's works passed as perfectly orthodox even after his condemnation for heresy, when published under the name of other authors whose views were regarded as orthodox. Nevertheless, inasmuch as his views on the Incarnation were a challenge in integral Christology, they could not find acceptance by the Church.

The belief in the pre-existence of the Son of Man goes further back than the early patristic efforts at formulating a Christology: it has its roots in pre-Christian Jewish times when ideas of a celestial figure 'like unto a Son of Man' (as in Daniel) were fairly widespread and, apparently, exercised a considerable influence on the messianism of the Pharisees. Ch. Harris in *Creeds or no Creeds* maintains that it is one of the most assured results of recent Synoptic criticism (liberal as well as orthodox) that the title 'Son of Man'

sophiology, more particularily in the idea of the Wisdom of God in which the archetypes of all things are ideally and potentially present, though as yet not possessed of external actuality.[1] To the mind of the Fathers who aimed at attaining the vision of a living unity of Christ's person, Christ is not a divinely animated man, nor one who, so to say, carries God within himself, but God who was made man. The Incarnation would have been a mere theophany or manifestation of God unless the entire person of Christ was as truly God the Word as the man Jesus, or unless God was also man and man was God. Being an *act* of God, the Incarnation involves intimate co-inherence, interchange and mutual appropriation ($\pi\epsilon\rho\iota\chi\acute{\omega}\rho\eta\sigma\iota\varsigma$, $\mu\epsilon\tau\acute{\alpha}\delta\sigma\eta$, $o\acute{\iota}\kappa\epsilon\acute{\iota}\omega\sigma\iota\varsigma$) of the human and the divine, in which each belongs to the other and is necessary to its completeness. And this inevitably faced the Fathers with the fact that the introduction of manhood into God testifies to an intrinsic compatibility and mutual relatedness between the two, in virtue of which Christ's manhood found its personality, or, to use a term devised by Leontius of Byzantium (sixth century), was enhypostatized in the person of the Son of God.[2] It is, indeed, not enough to content oneself with merely stating that certain things belong to a complete humanity and certain other things to a complete deity in Christ. The question is how Godhead and manhood can become one person; and unless this question is taken into account, the Incarnation cannot be shown to have really happened. The reality of Christ's manhood must therefore intrinsically point to God as its realization; and it cannot be represented as a thing standing side by side with, or related in a mere extraneous way to, another thing, namely God: that is to say, it must bear within itself the theandric potency of Incarnation. Thus it is that, on the one hand, the Son of God is

implies actual and personal pre-existence of the Messiah as a divine-human being in a state of glory and majesty with the Father in heaven (quoted by Charles Gore in *Belief in Christ*). See the critical examination of all the relevant evidence by Gore, ibid., Note C, 'The Belief in the Pre-existing Son of Man', and, more fully, by Lagrange, *Le Messianisme chez les Juifs*.

[1] See Sergius Bulgakov's *The Lamb of God* (in French as well as in Russian) which is the most powerful attempt at developing systematically the principles of theandrism with reference to the teaching concerning Our Lord's person and work.

[2] Cf. Hilary of Poitiers, who brings out these ideas in the strongest and boldest possible expressions: *On Psalms*, lxvii. 25; *On Matth.* iii. 2; *On the Trinity*, ix. 14).

shown as revealing in the Incarnation once for all and once for
ever that which is eternally latent in His nature and, on the
other, the reality of the Word made man is traced back to the
nature of man; while human nature itself, and indeed the whole
creation, are seen as reaching their fulfilment in God-manhood.
And no *a priori* objections can be allowed to minimize the import of this theandric revelation.

A whole series of important conclusions must be drawn from
these Christological insights. To begin with, they exhibit the
universal significance of the incarnation of the Son of God to
the entire human race. Since human nature in its entirety is re-
born and united with God in Christ, something is potentially
done not merely *for* but *to* and *in* mankind as a whole (as is,
indeed, explicitly stated by Irenaeus and, in particular, by
Gregory of Nyssa and Hilary of Poitiers). This in no way involves
a mechanical conception of the power of Atonement, whereby
we are, so to say, automatically drawn into Christ. It is through
faith and in freedom that we partake of the fruits of Christ's
Atonement. Nevertheless, God gives His saving grace not extraneously but through and in the humanity of Christ, to be
more precise, through and in his God-manhood: in other words,
man in his very manhood, is affected by the place he has taken
in Christ. This gives the lie to sectarian voluntarism or decision-
ism, which fails to see that decision itself presupposes an already
existing relation between him who decides and him in the face of
whom the decision is made: indeed, to *de-cide* is to confirm that
there can be ultimately no division. Grace, then, proceeds not
only from Christ's Godhead but from his God-manhood, whose
eternal presence and operation in the world and in man is
effectuated by the Holy Spirit. It is, in this sense, not only a
divine but a human activity as well: it is human even in its
most terrifying transcendence. Everybody is therefore ordained
to and worthy of Christ's presence (except probably him who
thinks he is!). Men as mankind stand and fall together, and it is
each man's destiny to walk once at least with Christ to
Emmaus.

Furthermore, inasmuch as man is an historical being, the universal significance of the Incarnation must be extended to History as such. In the hypostatic union of God and man the divine
and the human for the first time reached the predestined goal.
The drama of the Incarnation takes possession of Time, reveals

the meaning of Time and transforms it into History, since the Character in this drama is entirely of Heaven and entirely of Earth, of Eternity and of Time. Christ is the Beginning and the End of Time, or, one may say, the Centre of History, for, as a fact of History, He must be understood in His relation to what went before and what followed after. He is thus the turning point of the historical order: He is, as it were, the once-for-all-instant of creative divine-human fulfilment, from out of which the flow of Time, of past into present and future acquires meaning: from which, therefore, everything flows backward and forward.[1] Yet this very fulfilment of Time is possible because Time does not engulf Christ, because He transcends Time: it is measureless in its extent and measureless in its fount and centre—it is God self-offered 'before the foundation of the world'; in the manger; in the Upper Room; on Calvary; in the 'empty tomb'; in cloven tongues like as of fire; and on the Great White Throne. . . .

If the eternal Son of God could make the human His own and constitute it a determination of Himself: that fact illuminates the whole relation of God towards His creatures. If, as we have found, there is an essential relatedness between the human and the divine in Christ, the Incarnation must be deemed the revelation in History of the eternal creative movement in the inmost depth of divine life. This does not take anything from the finality of the Incarnation, since the revelation is not a mere manifestation, one of many manifestations even if the supreme one, but an act and an activity whose power is based alike on what God *is* and *does* in Christ. And precisely because Christ is not a mere human manifestation of the divine which itself remains aloof and changeless behind such manifestations, but the mystery of God's (and man's) supreme self-engagement, the Incarnation must be deemed an absolutely unique, decisive and unrepeatable event.

God's infinite perfection may demand His absolute self-sufficiency: but this cannot be understood in an abstract man-

[1] I am unfortunately not competent to discuss the problem of what this absolutely unique event in and for Time can signify, if we consider that the earth on which it occurred is 'one of a myriad myriad floating specks of dust' and that life on earth is an 'accident'. We are, however, dealing with a metaphysical, not a scientific, question. There are some interesting suggestions about the appearance of the earth and life on it in James Jeans's *The Mysterious Universe*.

ner. In point of fact His perfection rises above the abstract logical incompatibility between an incommunicable, self-contained being and a communicable being.[1] God *is* Love: that is to say, love is not a mere attribute of God; it is not 'a nice thing about him', but His very life. And this signifies the union of self-sufficiency and self-communication. A love which in giving does not assert itself is an impersonal emanation, and a love which is in no way related to or affected by the beloved and merely returns upon itself in perpetual self-confrontation and self-satisfaction is conceitedness and narcissism. The fact that God appears as Creator, Saviour, Redeemer, and, indeed, as the suffering God who takes upon Himself the sins of the world is not an additional activity in which He is engaged in a supplementary way but the revelation of His Godhead. No true vision of God can, therefore, be attained unless the elements of self-sufficiency and self-communication are seen as intimately and inextricably co-inhering and interpenetrating. Such a vision however spells abandonment of the Aristotelian and, generally speaking, Hellenic theism for the sake of the Hebrew image of God. It is the great dividing line between Hellenism, for which History does not really matter, whether from the 'point of view' of God or of man, and Christianity with its inherent affirmation of the supreme meaning of History.[2] Likewise, and on the same grounds, we must repudiate the classic view which dissociates necessity and freedom in God. On this view, to use the language of scholastic theology, God, being the infinite good and knowing Himself as such, loves Himself necessarily with a love adequate to the object, that is, with an infinite love, while He loves His creatures not necessarily but 'arbitrarily' or 'accidentally'. But this view is a sheer abstraction: it ignores or invalidates what is the pre-eminent characteristic of absolute love, namely an integral personal relation which knows no alternatives and

[1] This is expressed in the Orthodox teaching, formulated by Gregory Palamas, concerning God's 'being' and 'energies' which, though distinct, are integrated in the unity of the transcendent-immanent life of God. See on this Vladimir Lossky's *Théologie Mystique de l'Eglise d'Orient*.

[2] It is significant that the phrase 'I am that I am' in Exodus iii, 14, which is usually quoted as the biblical witness *par excellence* of God's 'necessary being', is, in fact, less a revelation of his self-sufficiency than a divine promise: 'He will be with them, helper, strengthener, deliverer; the word is explained by the "I will be with thee" of verse 12' (A. H. McNeile, *Exodus*, Westminster Commentaries, p. 22).

which, by being a personal relation, is *ipso facto* a correlation, involving mutual relation in freedom.[1]

Love is not a mere tendency towards a good in virtue of which the world becomes a kind of mirror wherein God perceives His own beauties and plays with Himself; nor is it a divine way of capriciously disposing of one's creatures, but precisely and essentially a personal relation which, far from implying either arbitrariness or necessity, reveals the passing of God's inmost life into inequality with Himself, into His other one, that is to say, a reciprocal activity which cannot be expressed in any rationalistic terms, whether those of abstract necessity or of equally abstract and empty *liberum arbitrium*. God, then, is and dwells entirely in Himself and yet exists for that which is other than Himself.

The assumption, however, of a correlation and even connaturality between God and man which underlies the Christological fact of God-manhood cannot be construed into a monophysitism or pantheism which merges the human and the divine: this would, in fact, render meaningless the very question of divine-human relations which imply the existence of two distinct orders of being each of which is a reality not resolvable in the terms of the other. The Incarnation signifies that 'only in so far as Christ is at every moment divine can he be at any moment truly human'.[2] Only because He is the eternal Word of

[1] The differentiation of freedom and necessity, when applied to God, seems to be altogether beside the point, for freedom and necessity in God are no states extraneous to one another and cannot be regarded as mutually exclusive. God's unity transcends all such differentiations. An analogy may be seen in human love where particularity, inequality and distinctiveness become a medium for a supreme and most intimate unity, which is at once necessary and free.

[2] This is the principal thesis of one of the most important recent Christological studies in English by H. M. Relton (*A Study in Christology*). Relton maintains even that Christ was man *because* He was God, that His manhood would have been incomplete if it had possessed a human self only. There is patristic evidence for such an emphasis. The main defect of Relton's exposition is that he tends to identify consciousness and personality (though, admittedly, an impersonal consciousness is a difficult notion), as others before and after him identified will and personality: he does not seem to be able to transcend purely psychological terms when treating of Christ's God-manhood. Lionel Thornton in a great Christological work writes: 'The human organism is not less human because it is taken up into union with the eternal Logos and has become the organ of his deity. Just the reverse' (*The Incarnate Lord*).

Only after the present essay was finished did Eric Mascall's recently published book, *Christ, the Christian and the Church*, come into my hands. This

God by whom all things were made can He be in His incarnate state 'the hypostatic centre of a perfect manhood in every conceivable relationship in which that manhood stands to God and to other creatures' (Relton). His transcendence is therefore the presupposition without which there can be no possibility of His living a truly human life.

At this point arises once again the problem of God's self-limitation which led us to the discussion of the idea of God-manhood.

To assert the fact of God's self-limitation is not to dictate what God must be in His relation to the world, but first and foremost

stimulating contribution to the Christological discussion contains an important critique of some modern Christologies (including that of Relton) as well as a constructive treatment of the traditional teaching concerning Christ's person. Its avowed aim and its real merit is to bring out the ontological basis of the Chalcedonian dogma over against the 'psychologism' of modern Christological constructions, particularly modern kenoticism. After all, Christology is concerned with the question Who is Christ and not What it feels like to be Christ. My main criticism of the book with regard to the subject under discussion may be summarized, though hardly made sufficiently intelligible in a footnote, as follows: 1. Any illustration of the co-existence of Godhead and manhood in Christ in terms of different functions exercised by a single human individual—a key-illustration in Fr. Mascall's constructive exposition—is not only limited in its application, as all illustrations are, but actually misleading. In this illustration the problem underlying the Christological dogma of two distinct spheres of being, God and man, united in a single personal existence is completely blurred. Manhood cannot in any sense be regarded as a 'function' of Godhead. At very best this merely states a fact which constitutes the problem. St. Gregory of Nazianzus has some very damaging remarks on such and similar illustrations. 2. To say, even though backed by St. Thomas's authority, that the incarnation in relation to the Word of God is not in Time is to reduce it to a mere manifestation in which God remains external to the Incarnation and does not enter the realm of History: in other words, it is a virtual annulment of the Incarnation. 3. Fr. Mascall's emphasis on the fact that the unity of Christ is brought about 'not by the conversion of Godhead into flesh, but by taking up manhood into God' (*Quicunque vult*) does not eliminate the problem of *kenosis* but, on the contrary, affirms it. This fact must be seen in conjunction with the other biblical and credal witness about God *coming down* to earth and *becoming* man. There is no question here of 'either—or' but one of 'and—and', to use Fr. Mascall's own motto. In Christology we have to deal throughout with what has just been called the correlation of two distinct spheres of being, divine and human, in the one person of the Son of God. It seems that Fr. Mascall underestimates or even evades the issue involved, whereas Gore, Matthews, Relton, and Weston, whom he criticizes so acutely, have faced it boldly, even if, admittedly, sometimes on wrong assumptions. It is significant that the depreciation of *kenosis* is most prominent in Arianism and semi-Arianism which marked the intrusion into Christendom of the Classical spirit of Aristotle. The story of St. Athanasius shows where the Church stood in this conflict between the Gospel and Hellenism.

to show what the Christian facts assert of themselves.[1] It is to do justice to the supreme act of God's revelation in the world and in man, which is expressed in the second clause of the Creed: '...for us men and for our salvation came down from heaven'. Now it is hardly necessary to explain that this does not refer to any spatial, astronomical occurrence, as though 'heaven' were above earth in space, but to a metaphysical event in which 'descent' signifies an act of condescension from out of the transcendent realm of being into that of creaturely existence, thus involving self-restraint, self-humiliation, *kenosis* on the part of God. 'Christ Jesus, who being in the form of God ($\grave{\epsilon}\nu$ $\mu o\rho\phi\hat{\eta}$ $\theta\epsilon o\hat{v}$) thought it not robbery to be equal with God: but made himself of no reputation and took upon him the form of a servant ($\grave{\epsilon}\kappa\acute{\epsilon}\nu\omega\sigma\epsilon$ $\mu o\rho\phi\grave{\eta}\nu$ $\delta o\acute{v}\lambda o\nu$) and was made in the likeness of men: and being found in fashion as a man, he humbled himself ($\grave{\epsilon}\tau a\pi\epsilon\acute{\iota}\nu\omega\sigma\epsilon\nu$), and became obedient unto death, even the death of the cross. Wherefore God also hath highly exalted him, and given him a name which is above every name: that at the name of Jesus every knee should bow, of things in heaven and things in earth, and things under the earth; and that every tongue should confess that Jesus Christ is Lord, to the glory of God the Father' (Phil. ii, 6–11; cf. 2 Cor. viii, 9). An intense and varied controversy was evoked by these well-known Pauline words which describe the act of the Son of God in taking our manhood: so much so that it would hardly be convincing to base any definite theory of God's self-limitation upon biblical or, for the matter of that, upon patristic foundations of a precarious nature.[2]

---

[1] On this point see Oliver Quick's *Doctrines of the Creed*, Part 2, ch. xiii, p. 134 ff.

[2] On the whole the Fathers were primarily concerned with the question of God's impassibility and did not devote much attention to the implications of Christ's *kenosis*. Nevertheless, true to the New Testament, they did acknowledge the fact of divine humiliation in the Incarnation, and they did ask questions as to the relation of this humiliation to those cosmic and providential functions of the Son of God which He exercises eternally in His divine being. Indeed, they even saw that in some sense it must be possible to refer sufferings to the Word of God, since otherwise Christ could not be recognized as having really put Himself in our place; that He could not have conquered sin unless He was no mere man that suffered. Thus Irenaeus, in emphasizing the reality of Our Lord's human experiences, acknowledges a 'quiescence' of the divine Word 'while he was tempted and dishonoured and crucified and slain'. Ambrose refers to the ideas of some, as he puts it, 'less timid than himself' (!) who affirm that Christ could both grow in knowledge and be ignorant of the future. Theodoret boldly protests against attempts to minimize or to explain away the explicit witness of the New Testament: 'If he (Christ)

The Beginning and the End

It would be even more presumptuous to argue the idea of *kenosis* from abstract metaphysical presuppositions. Rather it should be based upon the very fact of the Incarnation, which involves a self-humiliation on the part of God, whatever theory we may adopt as to its mode of realization.

We must repeat, in opposition to some of the more extreme modern kenoticists who go so far as to conceive of a divine suicide in the Incarnation and thus end in a *reductio ad absurdum* of the very idea of *kenosis*, that only 'in so far as Christ was at every moment truly divine could he have been at any moment truly human'.[1] There can, indeed, be no question of *kenosis* at all unless there is present throughout the subject of such *kenosis*; unless, that is to say, Christ is throughout the God-Man. Christ is 'whole in what is his, whole in what is ours' (Leo's *Tome*); and the question of His *kenosis* is not one of extent but one of intensity, not one of a static condition but one of a dynamic relationship: that is to say, He is not found as devoid of certain constituents of His divinity but as one who is wholly God and Man in His very *kenosis*, in which the Godhead is, as it were, contracted to the measure of His humanity, and the humanity exalted to the measure of His divinity. And the more intense

knew the day and, wishing to conceal it, said he was ignorant, see what blasphemy is the result of this conclusion: Truth tells a lie' (ἡ γαρ ἀλήθεια ψεύδεται.) Hilary, in discussing God's self-manifestation under human conditions, has some striking passages about the divine 'self-emptying' (*evacuatio formae Dei*); and Cyril states that 'God let himself down to the limit of the self-emptying' and 'suffered the measures of humanity to prevail in his own case'. Gregory of Nyssa recognized that a merely human death could not be the death of death and insisted that the Logos was truly humbled and truly took part in sufferings, not merely by appearing to suffer or to die. Finally, Leontius of Byzantium took with great emphasis the side of the *agnotae* and declared, not without some exaggeration, that almost all the Fathers held to Our Lord's ignorance. But the most outstanding patristic witness to the reality of *kenosis* belongs to Gregory Thaumaturgus, who deals with the question in the wider context of the capacity of God for suffering (see his *Dialogue with Theopompus*, edited in Joannes Pitra's *Analecta Sacra*, Patres Anteniceani). He proceeds from the assumption, which underlies our own argument also, that God's will cannot be opposed to His nature, and that suffering can and must be predicated of God when the experiences which He takes upon Himself are directed by God's love to a good end, and show no frustration on the part of God but His mysterious inward power which is revealed even in Christ's mortal agony. (For more patristic texts see Gore's *Dissertations on Subjects connected with the Incarnation*.)

[1] Generally speaking, modern theology as reflected in all the recent conflicting Christological theories does not seem to have gone much beyond the same positions which confronted the Fathers who had to meet the challenge of Nestorian dualism on the one hand and Eutychian monism on the other.

the *kenosis* the more real must be the divine otherness of Christ. In this sense the humanity of Christ is fundamentally something assumed and appropriated—the humanity, namely, in which His Godhead is limited and depotentiated; although, as we have seen, it is no mere external addition or a non-essential transitory thing pertaining to His Godhead.

The truth, then, for which kenotic theology contends is the reality of Christ's manhood, which determines what limitation God must undergo in order that He may live a truly human life. True, this limitation of God is an act of freedom, of eternal self-identical love by which the Word of God deigned to enter upon manhood and to face to the uttermost all the consequences of that act. But it was actualized not by the Word's arbitrary extraneous adjustment to, but by His real co-inherence with, by His becoming the real subject of, human existence, and by His submitting Himself to its conditions.

Chapter IV

THE HISTORICITY OF JESUS CHRIST

We must now turn to some problems concerning the 'Jesus of History' which have of late preoccupied the consciousness of men, more so than in the time when Christendom lived by a direct awareness of the image of Christ made not with human hands and by endeavouring to express that image in its own theological language. But, although modern man has lost this awareness to a large extent, he nevertheless remains profoundly disturbed by the problem and mystery of Jesus. Indeed human consciousness persists in being intensely concerned with the perennial question: Whom do men say that I am? And the attempts to apply the methods and achievements of modern historical science to the problem of the historicity of Jesus were, no doubt, provoked by the challenge contained in that question, even if such attempts proved, in the last resort, a failure and have only served to enhance man's uneasiness and disquiet.

Two opposite tendencies may, roughly speaking, be distinguished in the investigations concerning the problem of the historical Jesus.[1] Both tendencies issue from and lead to a denial of the integral truth of Christ's God-manhood. But they arrive at opposite conclusions, and it is extremely edifying to follow up these investigations, in spite of the fact that, or, perhaps, because, they drive us into blind-alleys. None of them have helped to bring about a meeting with the real God-Man Jesus Christ. One way led to a denial of the fact of His Godhead, while allow-

[1] The most adequate work on the history of the subject is probably still Albert Schweitzer's *The Quest of the Historical Jesus* (English translation). Schweitzer was himself a representative of the 'apocalyptic' school, which depicts Jesus as a prophetic enthusiast convinced of the immediate arrival of the world catastrophy and the Kingdom of God in which He Himself is to ɩeign. See also Charles Gore, *Belief in God*, and Digges la Touche, *The Person of Christ in Modern Thought*. The problem underlying the two tendencies under discussion is the subject of a most penetrating analysis by N. Berdyaev in his *Dialectique existentielle du divin et de l'humain*, ch. I and VIII.

The Historicity of Jesus Christ

ing the existence of His (mutilated) manhood. The other led to a denial of the fact of His manhood, while in a sense acknowledging the existence of a discarnate divine Logos.

Scholars representing the former tendency have their roots in the eighteenth-century Enlightenment. Their original concern, shared by many minds to-day, was to strip the Gospel story of every element of the miraculous by giving rather grotesque interpretations of the Gospel miracles and, generally speaking, to eliminate the fact of God's coming into the world of History and Nature by adjusting the story of Jesus to their rationalistic presuppositions. In doing so they and their successors did not completely break all ties with traditional Christianity, and they managed to save the remnants of the historical Jesus in the form of an inspired religious teacher. Nevertheless the result was a stunted rationalistic and moralistic faith, a set of ethical principles, which eventually brought about a complete loss of vision even of the 'Jesus of History'. Such to a great extent is the religion of Harnack. [1] The fact of Christianity, the birth of the faith in Christ as God, Saviour and Redeemer, remained utterly beyond the pale of this critical school, which, moreover, tended to treat the existing Gospel records rather unscrupulously, even though it may have performed a necessary task of textual criticism.

The other tendency, the denial, that is, of the historical fact or facts concerning Jesus Christ, goes back likewise to the eighteenth century; and although there are few who would advocate it at present in its original form it is of considerable importance in its implications. One of the first representatives of this school was François Dupuis, who declared that Christ is a 'solar myth'. The idea of the mythological character of Christ won the day in some critical quarters. It was revived by David Strauss, whose publication of the *Life of Jesus* towards the middle of the last century received both very wide popularity and condemnation. He made an attempt to reconstruct the life of Jesus on the assumption that a myth-creating process took place in the early Christian community. [2]

[1] See his *Das Wesen des Christentums*, where Jesus Christ appears as a gentle figure, preaching a pietistic religious sentimentalism, a lofty morality, inspired by the idea of God's fatherhood and the equality and brotherhood of men, and healing the sick by a kind of suggestion. See also the somewhat different version of the same in Bousset's *Kyrios Christos* and in Kirsopp Lake's *Landmarks of Early Christianity*.

[2] Strauss's theory of the formation of the Gospel myths was combated

The Beginning and the End

The mythological theory started, as a rule, from the hypothesis that the Gospels represent not a story, in the sense of an historical account, but rather tales about a mysterious god or theological and mythological treatises expressing the beliefs of the primitive Christians. The theory was particularly favoured by those who were anxious to strike a blow at the Christian faith, and it commended itself as a most radical and apparently irrefutable objection to Christianity, in comparison with which all the other remonstrances seemed weak and unimportant. There ensued a competition in the radicalism of denying the historicity of Christ. The 'Lives of Jesus' in the manner of Renan became a thing of the past and came to be regarded as a literary nicety.

The most radical representative of this mythological school was Arthur Drews.[1] An adept of the philosophy of Eduard Hartmann, Drews objected to the historicity of Christ on the philosophical, rather than historical, grounds that a religion of 'pure spirit' does not admit any form of 'religious materialism'. He was prepared to acknowledge the existence of Christ as a discarnate divine Logos but not as one who dwelt among men on earth and in History. To describe Christianity as a religious materialism was, no doubt, perfectly correct, inasmuch as its truth is revealed in and based on certain unique events in Time and Space; but for Drews this was a sign of a vicious Semitic infection, and he rejected it in the name of an anti-Semite 'aryan' spiritualism. His position was diametrically opposed to the 'Nestorianism' of the other modern critical school, the modernity of which, however, is no less senile than the Drewsian 'Monophysitism'. In both cases we are confronted with a definite dissolution of the divine-human image of Christ, a dissolution which is inevitable on the Procrustean bed of the 'either purely historical or purely super-natural'.

later by Bruno Bauer, who purported to prove that a whole series of evangelical stories had been fabricated by the authors themselves. The controversy between these two was carried out in the philosophical guise of a battle between Hegelian 'self-consciousness' and 'substance'. The question whether the miracle stories of the Gospels came into being through an unconscious myth-creation within the community or whether they were made up by the evangelists themselves was magnified into the question whether substance or self-consciousness was the decisive driving force in world-history. This was followed by Max Stirner, the prophet of solipsism, with his substitution of the sovereign Ego for self-consciousness.

[1] See his *Die Christusmythe*.

The Historicity of Jesus Christ

The apologists of Christianity were considerably alarmed by the mythological theories. But they, no less than their opponents, missed the point in their refutations. The fact is that no biography of Jesus can be construed at all with the current means and methods of historical criticism. There is, it would seem, no absolutely convincing argument against the contention that the data for such a biography are a product of mythological processes or of theological thought within the early Christian Church. The non-Christian sources, on the other hand, Jewish and Roman alike, are too insignificant to provide a certain basis for the establishment of the historicity of Christ. In the face of this state of affairs believers and unbelievers alike were guilty of confusing the issues, of jumbling two orders of being and hence employing a wrong method of historical inquiry. The facts and truths concerning Jesus Christ cannot depend primarily on either the positive or the negative results of historical criticism, since they have a transcendent as well as an immanent source. This in no way suggests that we must take refuge in the subterfuge of 'double truth', but it does mean: put off thy shoes from off thy feet, for the place whereon thou standest is holy ground! The science of historical criticism itself shows an awareness of this situation, and proves it by nothing more than its very helplessness, its constant ups and downs and oscillation between extremes.

It must be emphasized that the establishment of the existence of a mythological process, of a creative activity within the Christian Church was a discovery of paramount importance and showed a great insight on the part of the scholars who made it. This fact in no way prejudges the answer to the question as to whether this process or activity concerns objective realities, or is merely a matter of deliberate human arrangement and of illusions. Elsewhere it has been pointed out that, contrary to the current mode of speech, a myth is not a mere fable but the symbol of certain objective facts and events, and that mythological thinking is much more adequate for the expression of ultimate realities than conceptual reasoning and ratiocination. Science has, therefore, no right or reason whatsoever to declare *a priori* that a myth is a lie or, objectively speaking, an unreality.

What, then, does it signify when it is asserted that the primitive Church was engaged in creating myths? It means nothing more or less than the recognition of the life of Church-tradition,

in which and through which Christians touch on and enter into the deepest ultimate realities. The truth concerning the God-Man Jesus Christ is known not externally, by subjecting the remains of extant or imaginary past monuments to scientific observation, but first and foremost from within, through sharing in the life of tradition which is of Time and yet transcends the breaches made by Time. The empirical forms of tradition depend of course on more or less external circumstances, on place, language, national character, and so forth, but it is no mere archeological memory which fills up the chinks of past and present, nor, indeed, an extraneously imposed law or norm, but the very life of the Church; and these forms become transparent to the Word of God who renders them the operative meeting-place between Himself and man. The work of biblical criticism has served mainly to show the void of man's isolation, to alienate and divorce man from the history of Christ. Through sharing in the life of tradition, on the contrary, we commune and unite our individual lives with the mystery of God's revelation in Time which is the essence of all History. It is not easy for modern man to realize the true value of tradition. He throws off tradition easily for his own personal convenience. He tends more and more to become the victim of sheer activism, which bases all existence on the worship of each present moment, and fails to realize that the present is meaningful only in self-transcendence and is, as such, pregnant with past and future; or else he falls a victim to futurism, which is based on the cult of evolution and uses Time as a mere means for the realization of abstract values. Both tendencies are heresies against History which is the realm of divine-human activity. Now, since Christian tradition pertains to the life of the Church, it is only within the Church that we can perceive and know and live the integral image of Jesus Christ, of God and Man in their unity and co-inherence.

It is significant that none of the great or small personalities of the past has ever evoked doubts as to his historicity. No one has seriously undertaken to compose treatises on the historicity of Cromwell or Napoleon; and doubtless there is much more empirical evidence about even the most unimportant historical personages than about Jesus Christ, who is yet the very turning-point of History and, as the calendar testifies, the initiator of a new era in human existence. We can sympathize with Renan's profound regret to have chosen for his studies a

class of researches *qui ne s'imposera jamais*. We are unable to write a biography of Jesus as we can in the case of so many other men and women whose existence has not had the slightest influence on world events; and the only real Life of Jesus, as recorded in the Gospels, is not a biography, just as an icon is not a portrait. The truth, however, is that the empirical unconvincingness of Jesus Christ is the greatest witness in favour of his reality: it is a witness to his supremely transcendent character. Christ's presence in History sets, therefore, a final limit to historical criticism, a limit of which the most conclusive proof is the possibility of denying his historicity.

The 'convincingness' of Christ's coming is revealed not in the external world of nature but in History. Now History, as we have seen, is the realm where two orders of being meet and interpenetrate. And it is in Christ that this meeting and interpenetration is accomplished. The Son of God came into Time, but the true dimension of this coming leads us beyond the external happenings of Time; it is perceived in the life of the Church, which is the everlasting active presence of Christ in the world—the Body of Christ bearing the signature of both the divine and creaturely orders of existence and embracing the fulness of being.

The empirical undemonstrability of Christ brings us, once again, face to face with the fact of *kenosis* and self-limitation which underlies God's relation to the world, and which is bound up with the freedom of man and the ambiguities of Time (see above). The Saviour of the world did not appear in Rome, the centre of world-civilization, where all the great historical happenings were focused. He was born of a small nation and lived on the roads and hills of a land whose importance appeared to be quite negligible; nor was there anything remarkable in the life of Jesus Christ from the point of view of Graeco-Roman civilization: it was a story of the failure of a 'religious teacher', belonging to a 'despicable race' who died the infamous death of crucifixion. It was all foolishness and infatuation in the eyes of the Graeco-Roman world, unworthy of attention, except perhaps as a matter for contempt and mockery.[1] They utterly

---

[1] There is a famous pagan cartoon representing a crucified human figure with the head of an ass. On one side another figure is depicted lifting its head in a gesture of adoration. Underneath there is written: 'Alexamenos adores his god'!

failed to realize that Truth is Truth only because and in so far as it is nailed to the cross; that the final *kenosis* on the cross is the utmost limit to which it is possible to go in testifying to Christ's divine-human reality. It is only in the new History, initiated in a tiny 'upper room' of Jerusalem, shown in tongues of fire—in the Church, the mysterious divine-human Body of Christ, which is in the world and yet not of the world—that was revealed the true image of Christ: unseen and yet pressing towards visibility, weak and yet victorious. Herein lies the 'riddle of Jesus' with which stricken and doubting man is wrestling. The meeting and co-inherence of two worlds and 'two natures' in a single divine-human life is indeed beyond the reason of a world where division and estrangement reign supreme.

These suggestions can in no way be construed into a kind of monophysite or docetic other-worldliness which dismisses Christ's manhood or assumes that his life upon earth was illusory; nor do they imply indifference to the historical Jesus. Such an inference would in fact run counter to the whole argument of the present essay. But to assert that Christ is as truly man as He is truly God does not eliminate the existence of two orders of being: that which is revealed in History and that which pertains to external nature. In the realm of History there are also present 'two natures', divine and human, and the human is no less real than the divine. The realm of nature, on the other hand, is real only inasmuch as it is integrated into History and ceases to be a domain of externality; it is real 'by derivation', in other words, its reality is essentially *symbolic*. The 'natural' life of Jesus Christ is a symbol; but it is no less real for that or illusory, as is taught by docetism in various guises. His natural life reveals and symbolizes a prime reality pertaining to the order of transcendence, just as the life of this world of ours is a realm which symbolizes transcendent reality. In Christ there is disclosed once for all a meeting and interpenetration of the two orders, of reality and symbol. The recognition of this reality does not, however, proceed from a perception of its symbolization and cannot be based on proofs derived from such symbolizations. The reverse is true: we perceive symbols through awareness of the reality which is symbolized in and through them, or we perceive symbols because we are aware of the symbolized reality.[1]

[1] This is admittedly a Platonic approach. But the insights of Platonism,

The Historicity of Jesus Christ

The fact of Jesus Christ is therefore known not from the fragments of external data but by an inward identification in the depth of History, in and through the experience of the Church. This experience transcends the disputes and controversies of all the schools of biblical criticism and cannot be based on any one of them. Doubtless we must and do acknowledge the value of these schools as a phase in man's attempt to know Jesus Christ; and we certainly cannot oppose them with a kind of falsified semi-science and with apologetics based on tendentious historical concoctions. The point at issue is of a different nature: namely, that our faith cannot and should not rely on mere fragments of external data. We have seen earlier on in our discussion of the problem of History that its true meaning is known through transcending the limits of Time, through a realization of their transcendent dimension. The meaning of the Gospel story and of the pathways of Jesus Christ on earth, in like manner, cannot be reached if we fail to transcend the flow of external temporal happenings which are the subject-matter of biblical criticism: it can be discerned only in the Church, in tradition, through entering into communion with realities of which these happenings are the operative symbol and manifestation—through a symbolism, in short, which, while delineating the two orders of being, neither reduces the natural world to mere appearances and prompts us to disembarrass ourselves from it nor isolates it within itself, but unites the two orders to one another. This symbolism leads us into dimensions which demand another vison than that which is at the disposal of empiricist historians.

partial as they are, are an inherent element of true epistemology. The application of symbolism to the understanding of History is an important theme in Berdyaev's interpretation of History. I am much indebted to him in this section (see his *The Meaning of History* and the already cited *Dialectique existentielle du divin et de l'humain*).

Chapter V

PROVIDENCE DIVINE AND HUMAN

It is usual to draw a sharp distinction between the providential and the creative activity of God, as if these were two separate departments in the relations between God and the world. In point of fact, the terms 'creation', 'sustenance', 'government' cannot be viewed as different unrelated divine acts, but rather point to the fundamental mystery of God's presence at each and every point of the world's existence. The providence of God is nothing more or less than a continuing creation, an unceasing creative activity in the world. Any differentiation in this respect must be regarded as an abstraction, because we cannot conceive of relations between God and the world in which the act of creativity is one particular thing followed by another one, which is that of providence, as if God were a workman who first constructs a machine, and then puts it on to its course and proceeds to watch it. The world is at every moment of its existence God's immediate determination. God does not face a ready-made universe, but creates it ever anew. This does not imply an 'occasionalism' *à la* Malebranche, who assumed the continuous interposition of God, and treated created beings as affording only 'occasion' for divine operations, since God's creativity is co-extensive with the self-determination of free created beings. Neither does it mean that this creativity is equivalent to a perpetual production, at each moment, out of nothing—a view which would involve us into attributing to God a kind of 'evil infinity', into assuming that everything was perpetually annihilated and re-made at each moment: in which case life would be reduced to something like the apparent movement of figures on the cinema screen. Existence is not a series of similar things in rapid succession, and life is not a chain of unrelated successive phases produced momentarily by a *Deus ex machina*. Indeed it is the continuity of life which makes its discontinuity, its variety and complexity, significant. The fact of man's per-

Providence Divine and Human

sistence, or of the persistence of the world in man and of man in the world, as the same self from moment to moment, is that which alike enables him to be aware of himself as a self at all and reveals the steadfastness of God, Creator and Sustainer. There is nothing 'provisional' in God's creative, or, for the matter of that, providential, activity, but both are edged with the once-for-all-ness that underlies His very relation to the world. Creation must, therefore, be understood as a unique and irrevocable act which, being an act of love, has no other alternative. 'God saw everything that he had made, and, behold, it was very good. . . . And he rested on the seventh day from all his work which he had made.'

Nevertheless, the world is not a finished mechanism and cannot be handed over to mechanical necessity, and once called into being is thereby ordained to be and to become itself, to create itself ever anew in the power of its theandric, divine-human destiny. 'My Father worketh hitherto and I work' and 'the works that I do shall /ye/ do also; and greater works than these shall /ye/ do.' It is this that gives the world the fundamental character of change, of a process never repeating itself and leading always to something new. And though this process be rent by conflicts, though it embody a power to polarize, to divide or even to destroy, it is yet a movement in which the things that are thus polarized, divided and destroyed reach out creatively to their fulfilment. But 'it takes time', it takes the whole of History—*to the End*, to see its creative meaning. Hence the fundamental error of the Kantian or quasi-Kantian ideal of the world as a complete teleological system in which the whole appears as the unity of its members and the members as the differentiation of the whole; hence also the error of 'finalism', whether in the form of Leibniz's monadology or otherwise, which implies that created beings realize a programme previously arranged ('pre-established harmony'). To postulate the totality of the real as thus complete is to consolidate a 'block universe' in which Time and History are of no account. 'If Time does nothing it is nothing.' Yet, as we have seen already, Time (not abstract spatialized time but concrete Time and hence History) is the core of creaturely existence.

Providence, then, is not realized at one stroke, but is a continuous activity. True, it belongs to the entire destiny of the world, but this destiny is not external to the world and does not

merely hover over it; neither is it merely immanent: something which starts from nowhere and leads nowhere, that is to say, something that signifies nothing. Rather, this destiny is itself only real by virtue of God-manhood *in actu*, and God's purpose in the world becomes a reality through being a divine-human purpose. Most of the difficulties concerning the problem of divine providence are created by what are, in the last analysis, Christological heresies, objectifications which judge life by its 'loose and bleeding ends', which start with the creature cut loose from God or with the Creator unrelated to His creature. But that is an abstraction, since God is there all along and Himself, far from being an Absolute for whom nothing is potential or unaccomplished, 'aims at the unfulfilled', enters into a relationship with his creature which not only moves him to initiate the work of salvation, but to become the subject of human existence, of suffering and passion. Providence, therefore, is a theandric mystery which requires a world where God is active and where man is active too. In short this is not a block universe, nor one in which God's providence is exercised *ab extra* after the fashion of an earthly architect or moral governor who imposes his laws upon men, but a realm of divine-human activity—the realm of History. And freedom under God's providential care belongs only to him who no longer knows providence and History as an extraneous force, but begins to apprehend them as an inward event, as the expression of God's and his own freedom.

In this sense even evil, which arises out of freedom, does not lie outside the pale of God's providence: not on account of its being in any sense determined by God, but because His love, without losing itself, is able to surrender itself to the utmost uncertainty of the creature's freedom, while remaining sure to make even the world's stricken and sinful existence a realm of theandric destiny. Such indeed is the triumph of divine art (τέχνη θεοῦ), that in this character of love God surrenders and exposes Himself in Christ to the irrational potentialities of human freedom, and yet does it so that through this very surrender or *kenosis* love reveals its victory. We repeat: providence springs not from a unilateral divine counsel, but from human freedom also, by which God's activity conditions itself.

God, then, is engaged in a 'conative activity', in movement, effort, desire. We must admit this if the world is the domain of God's providence and not of fate, of divine-human synergism and

not of fixed eternal decrees, a domain, that is, in which values are created and realized. The world, therefore, must possess a real existence for God, and Time and History must enter into his life. It is true that God's eternal triune being cannot be externally dependent on Time; yet He is not a static Absolute but, precisely, the triune God who enters into a positive relation with and reveals Himself in the Time-process. His eternal being cannot be conceived of as a mere absence of Time, as the time-less immensity of acosmic pantheism which involves no movement because it contains everything necessary to itself at every moment of its existence, in the sense, for instance, in which all the properties of a triangle are present in the triangle at any given moment. Such an abstract divine absolutism would make History unmeaning—an impersonal, eventless manifestation of a static divine Necessity, or, possibly, the pointless game of a capricious deity. All monistic philosophy, Indian, Aristotelian, Neoplatonic, or Idealist, if consistent must needs arrive at a denial of History and of the whole created universe and acknowledge the sole reality of God. It ignores the central truth of existence—the truth of God-manhood. Already the Old Testament prophets show the possibility of atonement in the fact that God is involved in and experiences the sorrow and pain of human existence. Now the affirmation of Christ, the God-Man, as taking upon Himself the destiny of stricken humanity constitutes the supreme recognition that God Himself experiences the pathways of human History—unless indeed the whole Gospel-story be a farce or a masquerade. Creation, Incarnation, Redemption and eschatological fulfilment lie in the depth of the triune life of God, in the inmost relations of God the Father, the Son and the Holy Spirit.

This accounts for the attribution of divine providence in all its acts and functions to the three Persons of the Holy Trinity respectively as well as to the Trinity as a whole. There is a universal activity of God in the world which is generally assigned to the Father ('My Father worketh hitherto . . .'); but there is no providential activity from which the Son is excluded ('. . . and I work'). There is, however, a distinctive providential activity of the Son which pertains to the 'kingly office' of His mediatorial work, and which was inaugurated by God's supreme intervention in the incarnate manifestations and atoning work of Christ as consummated in the resurrection, ascension, and His

abiding presence 'in the Spirit' (see Matt. xxviii, 20; xi, 27; John xiv-xvii). Similarly, the Holy Spirit is in a specific sense the God of providence, the Lord and Giver of life—the bond of unity between the unseen and the seen in the whole 'economy' of created beings. Thus, wherever there is life, there is the triune mystery of God, the sacred, divine Triad which signifies fulness and the victory over strife and division. But such victory is won in self-surrender through love; and providence involves the *kenosis* not of the incarnate Lord alone, but, in some sense, of the whole Holy Trinity, of the Father who gives His only begotten Son, of the Son who accepts Calvary and identifies Himself with mankind, and of the Holy Spirit who, while requiring no mediation for His hypostatization but exercising divine functions in His own person, is yet God's 'consequential and conjunctive agent' (Gregory of Nyssa) in whom the drama of eternal love is brought to its fulfilment. The triune life of God is thus related in its self-revelation to the life of men and of the world.

If providence is a divine-human activity, what are we to say of the 'attributes' of God which are usually introduced into the doctrine of providence, particularly of his sovereignty, under which is customarily placed divine omnipotence and omniscience, that is, in the language of theological textbooks, 'the knowledge that foresees, the will that determines and the power that executes'? One must confess that, to use an old metaphor, it is not easy to swallow these and similar scholastic pills which chewed upon turn the stomach, particularly in view of the intolerably naturalistic language in which they are frequently couched. Moreover, it would lead us into a jungle of technicalities to join the intricate controversy that divides, for instance, Thomism and Molinism, or those which divided subsequent schools of thought. We have, however, already attempted to give a critical estimate of certain aspects of the controversy. The underlying issue is, no doubt, of real importance for an understanding of the problem of providence; and a way of meeting the issue is already contained in the preceding argument. The main point is that there can be no divine providential power or knowledge out of relation to History. Some theologians have regarded the presence of God in the world as His logical knowledge of everything apart from any real connection with anything (on the human analogy in which we have foreknowledge of somebody's action without being responsible for its

realization). But this entails a deism which virtually annuls the very fact of providence. Others have regarded God's knowledge as timeless, as a knowledge at one glance of the whole temporal order. Both views err in not relating the knowledge of God to human existence, and it is just this relation which is of decisive import. We must affirm the presence of God's activity throughout; yet this is a theandric, not a unilateral activity.

Acceptance of the position of theandrism cannot of course be compelled by logical demonstration which starts from the concept of an abstract divine Absolute. Such acceptance is itself in the last resort an act of freedom, of free consent, and hence an act of faith. Our language, therefore, cannot be that of deductive logic but must needs be mythological: that is to say, the language of revelation, which speaks of God as changing His mind, as delaying His judgment, as grieved or as rejoicing.[1] In short, it admits the possibility of real change in the course of History dependent on human action and thereby precludes a closed universe where God is fettered or man predetermined by divine omnipotence and omniscience. God cannot, of course, be thought of as inferring His knowledge from the facts and happenings in our lives: God, to use A. E. Taylor's metaphor, cannot be imagined as someone who 'calculates the course of events like a "Laplacean demon", from a multitude of differential equations'. If God knows a future event, he certainly knows it whether or not it is involved in a past event. We have no right to impose any conditions on divine consciousness or imagine that, simply because we cannot ourselves foresee the free acts of our fellow-men, God must be similarly defective in His knowledge. The nineteenth-century view of God as a half-blind demiurge pushing His way helplessly into the clear light of the self-consciousness of men is a solemn but somewhat silly mockery of man's true predicament, and, moreover, can hardly inspire anyone.[2] And yet, in point of fact, we can boldly and

---

[1] It is hardly necessary to point out that such predications do not denote *passiones* in the strict sense, that is to say, passive states; for God is never passive. Rather, they are part of God's loving, kenotic relation to the world, in which He limits *Himself* and thus becomes relatively passible. For a detailed theological and patrological discussion of what divine passibility does and does not mean see J. K. Mozley's *The Impassibility of God*.

[2] Such ideas are by no means exclusively characteristic of the nineteenth century. Man was always tempted to turn God into a figment of his little moral and intellectual ideas. 'Nothing would induce me', wrote John Stuart

paradoxically proclaim that God does *not* know the future. God is eternally Himself; He has no 'parts' or 'inhibitions' or frustrated capacities; whatever God *knows* He *does*, for His knowledge is no static condition of contemplation but absolute activity. If, therefore, God has endowed man with freedom and thus refused to determine human existence unilaterally, He has thereby in some sense surrendered or limited His knowledge, no less than His almightiness. But this surrender or limitation is a *self*-surrender and a *self*-limitation, a *kenosis*, which He Himself has accepted in love. And if it is asked how there can be in God's mind a subjective certitude with regard to the ultimate fulfilment of creation which involves the exercise of the creature's freedom and in respect of which there is, therefore, no assignable ground of certainty, one can only reply that this certitude is the certitude of love whose nature is to love freely and to love the free and whose victory is manifested even in and through defeat. The knowledge of God is not susceptible of further dogmatization; and even this argument aims at the *mode* of divine knowledge rather than at what this knowledge is.

In the self-limitation of God, as well as in the primordial fact of God-manhood, the Time-process becomes real to God. Christian philosophy of History thus assumes both the openness of the transcendent to History and the openness of History to the transcendent; it assumes their mutual relation or correlation. It sees History as a drama which is revealed and fulfilled in the life of God and in the centre of which stands the Incarnate Lord, perfect God and perfect Man, 'who has made both one, and has broken down the middle wall of partition' (Eph. ii, 15). The true significance of the Christian message lies in that it shows the reality and power of God's penetration into Time whereby the chain of Time is broken and Time made significant alike to the Creator and the creature. This is true despite the unceasing struggle between God and History, despite the recalcitrance of Time to Him and His constant effort to achieve victory over Time; indeed this very struggle presupposes an inward correlation of the two. The victory He seeks implies no annulment of Time or aloofness from it. The struggle itself is co-extensive with the historic destiny of God's creation. Man may become aware that God is not: and then he gains the knowledge

Mill, 'to esteem God if I were convinced that God did not recognize my moral ideas'!

of the horror and unbearable folly of his individual and historical predicament; he awakens, not perhaps to ultimate, but to penultimate knowledge. 'Si Dieu n'existe pas il faut en tirer jusqu'au bout les consequences' (Sartre). God cannot be suppressed at little cost: if He does not exist we must at least acknowledge the frightful human situation; and this signifies to lay bare the divine-human sources of existence.

It is only when we thus view providence that it ceases to be a rule of safety which takes away man's responsibility for his own and the world's destiny and keeps him secure under the wings of a good-natured divine benefactor—that travesty of faith in the God who did not spare His Son and gave man freedom to crucify Him. The same, in a sense, must be said of providence in regard to the world of Nature, which is far from being the happy domain of 'harmonious adaptation of means to ends' by a transcendent or immanent power. Nature too is imbued with irrational potentialities, born as she is of primeval chaos and possessing relative independence. She may appear majestically serene; but her real secrets are hidden. No despot, not the greatest evil-doer on earth, has ever wielded power with the cruelty and indifference of Nature. She gives little ground for lightheartedly rejecting the presence of all chance and irrationality in her or of making inferences concerning the goodness of God. But Christ entered the life of Nature as well as the life of men: He was crucified above her dark abysses, and the light that shines from the crucified and risen Lord is a light shining in the elemental Night of Nature.

This faith enables us to meet responsibly the formidable objections of 'dysteleology', or the caustic and more than justifiable scepticisms of all Voltaires who satirize an optimism which can accept the earthquake of Lisbon, or any other 'earthquakes' that engulf human life, with a light heart.[1] But it does

[1] Cf. the oft quoted words of Hume: 'Were a stranger to drop suddenly into this world, I would show him, as a specimen of its ills, an hospital full of diseases . . . a field of battle strewn with carcases, a fleet floundering in the ocean, a nation languishing under tyranny, famine and pestilence. To turn the gay side of life to him and give him a notion of its pleasures, whither should I conduct him? To a ball, to an opera, to court? He might justly think I was only showing him a diversity of distress and sorrow.' No doubt, physical as well as spiritual sufferings have sometimes profited men. But it is also true that there is profound, outrageous, incredibly outrageous suffering which kills the least and most unpretentious of hopes. How are we to explain such things? Hardly by declaring, as the Stoics, Cynics or Epi-

not remove the disquiet and the tension; it does not prompt us to construct harmonious systems which would round off the contradictions of life. For all that it reveals we shall, contrary to the counsels of the wise, not cease 'to laugh, to weep and to hate'. On the contrary, it will make us apprehend more deeply than ever the tears and groans and, indeed, the silence of humanity, more so than any clear and plain, well-grounded and proven explanations. Until faith in providence as mere beneficence, until all speculations concerning the teleological intentions of a 'first cause' in the vicissitudes of 'second causes' break down, the faith that reconciles us to God and to the world in face of every conceivable evil and the pain-ridden destiny of man cannot rise. This applies equally to the teleological concepts and laws of natural science and to any other pretensions of the human brain to explain pragmatically the confused ways of History. The faith in providence does not compete with science or, for that matter, follow in its heels or allow itself to be perpetually duped by it: it is itself an act which transforms the natural configuration of all things—not, however, by elevating them into a world of fairy-tales where unusual happenings occur and where the winds are tempered to the shorn lamb but by discerning the silent yet living image of God-manhood which, like a mysterious hieroglyph, is written across the face of all creation.

Having said this, we may assert what is evident to everyone who has known and experienced the reality of God's presence and providential activity in the baffling circumstances of life: all one's thoughts, fears, apprehensions, hopes and joys seem to rush to group themselves anew in relation to that reality, so that they are suddenly transformed into a distinct pattern, and a light plunging into them and holding them begins to illumine their irresistible onslaught, almost before one has consciously grasped the significance of the reality itself. Thus God turns His terrible, searching, loving gaze at human life and under this gaze man is exposed in utter helplessness and utter boldness.

cureans did, that pain cannot or should not affect man, that it was something 'indifferent': a wise and virtuous man must be happy even if he were burnt alive. Did not Plotinus, who was a very wise and virtuous man and who never wept or laughed in his life, teach that the death of friends and near ones did not matter?

Chapter VI

THE OLD AND THE NEW

Aristotle says that it is a sign of philosophic boorishness to demand proofs for all assertions. This is hardly to be denied. There is, nevertheless, a strange and persistent tendency in all the cognitive endeavours of men throughout the ages to arrive at reality by logical deductions. 'If', as Leo Shestov, who, admittedly, went very far indeed in his irrationalism, wrote, 'man could wring a single secret out of History and Nature by logic, one would be, perhaps, compelled to take his endeavours into very serious consideration, since "conquerors are not judged"; but we fail to· see in the results of logical deductions anything save generalities and more or less empty prattle.' The truth, no doubt, is that man deceives himself by inferring where he should be looking, listening and wondering. *Primum vivere deinde philosophari.* Life looks different and reveals deeper dimensions when seen with one's eyes and heard with one's ears: the key to a true understanding of History and of human existence is found in the substitution of vision for general principles, of individualizations for generalizations.

This means the acknowledgment of a true insight on the part of those who believed that the history of anything is a sufficient explanation of it, and that the nature of human existence is comprehended in this very existence and not outside of or above it in some abstract, immutable and unchanging reality, of which existence is believed to be a mere appearance. Such is the truth alike of Historicism and of Existentialism which no 'always-idealists' are really capable of invalidating. It has been said of late, and reiterated, that, owing to its apparently odious relativistic and nihilistic implications, Historicism is an evil which must be overcome at all costs. And yet the emergence of this school of thought was one of the greatest spiritual revolutions in the development of European thought. It has emancipated historical knowledge from the tyranny of general conceptions

and has enabled it to meet the challenge of a multitude of events and experiences which show that History is truly apocalyptic—a creative movement towards incalculable issues, and a testimony to the radical novelty of every human situation.

Men persist in being terrified of the creative and the inexplicable in History; they are afraid of acknowledging and facing the disruptions of the allegedly uniform processes of life. They describe such things as 'chance', which in their minds cannot, strictly speaking, exist or, at least, should not exist. But this attitude leads us away from reality. It is impossible to gain an understanding of the meaning of History if events are regarded as always and everywhere fundamentally the same, so that all one has to do in order to apprehend them is to apply certain metaphysical or teleological conceptions. Nor can events be understood as bound together by a changeless all-pervading and in all particular cases identical immanental law, causal or otherwise—an attitude familiar to natural science and also characteristic of the outlook of the Graeco-Roman civilization, which thought and lived in terms of immutable natural laws and firmly believed in the stability of human nature and, above all, of human reason, if only they be freed from ignorance and passion. All these views meet only the quantitative transformations in History, but fail to explain their peculiar, concrete and qualitatively distinctive character, the historical decisiveness of an event, a human life or the life of a nation, of a social and economic condition, of a creative achievement, or the impact of an age.[1] This is by no means invalidated by the immanentist

[1] Admittedly, these tentative criticisms apply in some measure to the modern representatives of the Historical school themselves, especially to the Idealist philosophers of History such as Windelband, Rickert, and even Max Weber and Troeltsch who, while denying abstract teleology and the primacy of physical laws, tend to establish other abstract terms of reference and see facts in their relation to a universally applicable transcendental system of values. The same is true to some extent, as we have seen, of Dilthey. On these and other problems of Historicism see H. A. Hodges, op. cit.; Ernst Troeltsch, *Der Historismus und seine Probleme*, also his article 'Historiography' in Hasting's *Encyclopedia for Religion and Ethics*; E. Rothacker, 'Logik und Systematik der Geisteswissenschaften' in *Handbuch der Philosophie*, Abteilung II.

The question as to the ultimate ground of the specific character of individual phenomena (*principium individuationis*) has preoccupied philosophy from the very beginning. It was one of the main factors that divided medieval philosophy into two distinct schools: on the one hand Thomism, where Form or Idea does not go beyond the generic (*quidditas*), and where individuality is seen as determined by matter (except in the case of angels); and

aberrations of some historicists, particularly of the German school as represented by Herder, Hegel, or Gierke, who, in a sense, anticipated the Nazi principles of racialism and state-idolatry and played into the hands of the Hitlerite *conquistadores*. There is very little indeed in common between the 'historic destiny' proclaimed in the demagogical outbursts of the Nazi leaders and the 'historic destiny' of Christian theandrism. If we question the validity of immutable universal principles, we do so on the basis of the transcendent, to be more precise, of the theandric meaning of History, while acknowledging at the same time that historical immanentism had been largely provoked by the unawareness of History implied in these principles.

There is a long and venerable tradition in Western thought, which emanates, more directly, from medieval sources and has produced many legitimate and illegitimate, religious and secular offsprings, according to which absolute primacy is ascribed to the objective universality of Reality. But abstract objectivism and universalism imperil human existence and spell death. The individualism and nihilism which pervade the mind of modern man are the fateful outcome of and penalty for a tendency to banish the existent, the concrete, the singular, the personal to the limbo of anonymous abstractions and conceptualizations.[1]

on the other hand Scotism, where Form is seen in the concrete particularity of a phenomenon (*haecceitas*). It is not easy to say precisely where the Eastern Fathers stand or would have stood had they been parties to the dispute. It is significant, however, that their theology is characterized by an intense personalism and that, as this is shown in a most illuminating recent patrological study, the most 'philosophical' of the Fathers, Gregory of Nyssa, explicitly recognizes the methodological priority and superiority of the ὅτι ἐστίν over the ὅ τί ἐστίν, i.e., of 'existence' over 'essence' or 'idea': 'la vie est au-dessus du désir, la présence (παρουσία) est au-dessus de l'image et le miracle de l'arrivée continue (ἐπιδημία) est au-dessus de la présence même en tant qu'elle tendrait à s'établir dans la durée et l'habitude' (Hans von Balthasar, *Présence et Pensée*. Essai sur la philosophie religeuse de Grégoire de Nysse.)

[1] This may require certain qualifications with regard to Thomism. Modern Thomists have argued that the philosophy of St. Thomas is eminently 'existential'. Etienne Gilson writes: 'Why, St. Thomas asks, do we say that *Qui est* is the most proper name among all those that can be given to God? And his answer is because it signifies "to be", *ipsum esse*. . . . The word "being" as a noun designates some substance; the word "to be"—or *esse*—is a verb, because it designates an act. To understand this is also to reach, beyond the level of essence, the deeper level of existence' (*God and Philosophy*). Nevertheless Thomist philosophy does not belong to the type of 'existential' thought. 'Existence' is, in fact, subsumed in 'essence': this is particularly evident in the Thomist theory of knowledge and in psychology. Knowledge

The Beginning and the End

God and man alike have come to be regarded as things to be manipulated in accordance with abstract ideas and ends which are neither human nor divine. There is an unmistakable continuity between the scholastic *semper distingendum est*, by virtue of which God and man were to become objects of intellectual manipulation and systematization, and the theory and practice of the disintegration of the atom, by which man is to exercise dominion over this spell-bound world of ours and incidentally lay it in ruins. What has been lost is the true subjectivity of God and man, their mysterious, concrete, unrepeatable, irreduceable personal image. Indeed existence is that which constitutes its most individual, truly subjective character, which, however, does not exteriorize or isolate it from other existences but maintains it in the tension of the concrete fulness of life. And divine creation and providence alike are pre-eminently acts of 'existentiality' and 'individuation'.

Truly historical thinking presupposes then a method of inquiry which is determined not by rationally demonstrable abstract systems or absolute and everywhere identical standards, but by affirming the uniqueness of existence in all its diversity and particularity whether good or bad—'the wisdom', as Hooker said, 'which is learned by tract of Time'.[1] True to this attitude we are compelled to resist the worship of unfleshly ideas and ideals, even the loftiest, which hover over the mind of men; and the knowledge

is viewed as fundamentally a process of abstraction from the concrete and particular ('intellectus non cognoscit seipsum per suam essentiam, sed per actum quo intellectus agens abstraihit a sensibilibus species intelligibiles'); and the soul is defined as throughout an *ens rationale*, involving a depreciation and depotentiation of its *infinitum in potentia*, of its irrational, illimitable character, even though it is, at the same time, described as containing all the 'lower' forms of existence. Hence St. Thomas's accentuated intellectualism with its characteristic objectivist tendency to conceptual determinations and limitations.

[1] It is interesting to note that Hooker, despite his attachment to the idea of Natural Law and his general conservatism, possessed a very deep sense of History, which is perhaps even one of the most important characteristics of his *Ecclesiastical Polity*. It is indeed possible to re-state the problem of Natural Law in a way which takes History seriously and meets the challenge of Historicism—a task which still awaits full consideration (see however *Natural Law*, A Christian Reconsideration, ed. by A. R. Vidler and W. A. Whitehouse; also V. A. Demant, *Christian Polity*). There is no doubt that for many the idea of Natural Law supplies the one factor of stability in a disintegrating world: as it were a raft to which the survivors of the wreck of modern society may cling. But this fact can also be interpreted as serving to emphasize the very forces that belie this idea, forces that have to be met with more powerful and more creative weapons.

of History is to us not an application of such ideas and ideals to the changing circumstances of life, nor, for that matter, a reconstruction of the past as an unbroken series of happenings tacked together by causality, but a 'wandering through human souls'.

We must ask ourselves once more if these considerations, which are part of the insights of Historicism and Existentialism, do not discard the decisive problem regarding the *significance* of the historical processes, the problem of their ultimate meaning and End; if they do not engulf man in, or leave him a tool of, the impersonal precipitate flux of Time, whereby he will cease to have any relation to the transcendent God, to *pray* and to turn his gaze to heaven. We have already argued at some length and on various occasions throughout this essay that no judgment on historical phenomena can be made without taking into account the fact of their transcendent dimension, that these very phenomena are unthinkable out of relation to the transcendent God, while at the same time God Himself is not unrelated to History, and the knowledge of God and divine providence are derived from the facts and events of History, in which God's eternal ends are realized. Such is the primordial mystery of God-manhood. We are thus confronted with what may well appear, from the point of view of deductive logic, a vicious circle: on the one hand History is to be interpreted by the character and extent of its relation to God, and on the other by the fact that God conditions His power over History, and in that sense derives His significance for History, by History itself. This circle, however, is more properly described as an antinomy, the antinomy of theandrism, which is inherent in the very nature of the problem before us. And it is precisely this antinomy which gives insight into the meaning of human existence and of historical situations and tendencies which, being what they are, make for transcendence.

(a) Past, Present, and Future

Man is easily inclined to be infatuated with the past and to assign to it a validity which in fact in no way pertains to it. He makes desperate attempts to evade a state of present uneasiness and disquiet and in so doing falls a victim of the belief that the past, the antiquated, is of absolute value; he regards the present

and the future as at best a new opportunity for conserving allegedly immutable values or, in more apprehensive moods, as their inevitable destruction: in fact, he fails to acknowledge the transitory, fleeting, evanescent nature of every past, however glorious it may have been. Such a tendency, which often aims at combating the evils of the present and manifests itself in various guises, in Protestant primitivism, Byzantinism, medievalism, and in the romantic hankering after a 'return' to all kinds of things which are believed to be the lost paradise, is based on a false estimation of Time, on the failure to understand the transcendent dimension of Time. It proceeds frequently from some tragic historical experience entailing great spiritual strain and betraying its weight in the desperateness of the reaction in which ones hopes to find relief. [1]

One of the most characteristic expressions of 'infatuation with the past' can be seen in the reaction of some to social revolutions, which confront them with the need of repenting and expiating the evil past which has necessitated a revolutionary change. In every revolutionary epoch there is a clash between the old order and the new brought about not so much by 'ideologies' as by 'psychologies' (and, no doubt, by vested interest). The new order endangers what the old claims to possess. Since in every such epoch the new order conquers first in some particular country and is, for the time being, embodied in that country (England in the seventeenth century, France in the eighteenth century, Russia now) it creates cleavages between the nations, of which the representatives of the old order appear as 'crusaders' (for 'Christian civilization' and the like); but it also creates cleavages within the particular national community which undergoes the revolutionary experience, cleavages in which the inevitable victims of the revolution disclaim the responsibility for its irruption and, in their historic unawareness, see in it the external violence of usurpation preying on the people whom they claim to represent. In point of fact they merely defend the old order which was cramping the expressions of the new forces released by the revolution. [2] In both

---

[1] This aspect of the problem has been shown in a remarkable way by Prof. Toynbee, who brings into relation the phenomenon of 'infatuation with the past' and cultural disintegration (*A Study of History*, vol. vi, 'Schism of the Soul': *Archaism*).

[1] This is particularly evidenced in the attitude of an *émigré* (e.g. the French *émigrés* at the turn of the eighteenth century, the Russian *émigrés* of the Communist revolution, or the *émigrés* of the various nationalities after

cases we have to deal with an historic instance of the failure to repent or, which is the same thing, with a failure to respond creatively to the challenge of History—a failure which would be pathetic if it were not sinister, because it prompts its victim to very energetic and equally pernicious activity.

The past as mere past is part of disintegrated Time and has no advantage whatsoever over the present or future from the viewpoint of History. 'The Spirit bloweth where it listeth': God has intervened in the past and will intervene in the future; that is to say, past, present and future are equally open to God. But, in their state of isolation and extraneousness, past, present and future alike pertain to the realm of fleeting Time. The mere fact that something is inherited from antiquity or handed down by our forefathers is by no means a guarantee of its validity and truthfulness, although such a heritage *may* be authentic tradition: tradition, which historical criticism may seek to discredit, but which is, as we have already seen, a victory over the corruptibility of Time and a revelation of the theandric meaning of History. But the conservatism which idealizes the past just because it is the past or clings to it out of sheer inertia and incapacity of facing the present and the future is a denial of Godmanhood, and issues from the belief in an immutable past or an abstract objective order of things which must needs be imperilled by every kind of change. Men's supreme task is then seen to consist in conforming to that order. Yet this belief spells idolatry; it is a figment and an illusion of the human brain incapable of meeting the disrupting and disintegrating forces of Time or of imbuing them with transcendent meaning.

the last war)—the historic mischiefmaker *par excellence*, of whom Joseph de Maistre, himself an 'antiquarian' but an unusually farsighted and intelligent one, said: 'Les émigrés ne peuvent rien faire; j'ajoute même, ils ne *sont* rien.' (*Considérations sur la France*).

Nicolas Berdyaev in speaking of revolutions says that they occur 'because creative activity becomes impossible'. 'A revolution always brings with it an avenger who performs the greatest cruelties and acts of violence. . . . But those on whom the revolution wreaks its vengeance and whose old wrongs have caused its abuses . . . cannot claim to be champions of righteousness as against its unrighteousness, for the revolution embodies a right as compared with their wrong. . . . Vengeance is hideous, but it is not for those whose wrongs have provoked it to denounce its hideousness. . . . A revolution, like every other great and significant event in the destinies of mankind, involves me and every one of us. . . .' (*The Destiny of Man*, pp. 263-4.) There are some equally revealing remarks on the nature of revolutions in Thomas Carlyle's *The French Revolution*.

The Beginning and the End

But the future too is ambiguous. There is a form of idolatry of the future which is often the penalty of desperately clinging to the past that has in fact already completely eluded man under the impact of the present, to the extent of depriving him of every hope of seeing it triumphant. This opens the door for illusory apocalyptic expectations of an order that would destroy the evils of the present and inspires a frentic and fanatical activity to bring about the desired thing. 'Futurism and archaism', writes Professor Toynbee, 'are, both alike, attempts to break with an irksome present by taking a flying leap out of it into another reach of the stream of Time without abandoning the plane of mundane life on earth'. They represent 'desperate sorties from a position of present discomfort and distress which neither of them has any longer the heart to hold.'[1]

The novelty of the future is as much or as little a guarantee of its validity as the antiquity of the past. But novelty *may* be a revelation of truth, a sign of creative fulfilment, while it may also be a betrayal of one's historic heritage and a refusal to share the responsibilities of History. When novelty is seen in terms of progress—either in the sense of automatic changes for the better by a gradual addition of Time, or in the sense of the expression of some absolute intelligence which progressively realizes itself therein—we are confronted with an optimistic necessitarianism which belies the true nature of History. This is not merely because, in point of fact, life can be obstructed and arrested, and manifests itself in exhaustion as well as in advance, in regression as well as in fresh movements; but because History is the realm of divine-human activity revealing the human, as well as the divine, power of freedom and initiative, without which it (History) becomes an extraneous force and providence a blind and insuperable fate. It is this, and this above everything else, that imbues change with a truly creative character. Man is a child of God; but he is likewise a child of Time: he becomes and creates himself unceasingly and thus fulfils his theandric calling. In this sense human life is eminently a dynamic progressive movement inspired by *amor futuri*.

God-manhood, then, illumines the real meaning of the changes that History and man in History undergo. Truth remains admittedly ever identical with itself, but its 'operation' changes and is dependent on whether and how man changes,

[1] Op cit., vol. vi, p. 97.

The Old and the New

falls, rises, falls again, is enriched and humbled by new insights, raises new questions or makes new decisions. And man is destined to receive the Christian revelation with or in the complexity of his changing awareness. There was a time when Galilean fishermen, risen we know not whence, were called upon to utter the Word of God. And there was also a time when the Word was uttered by the genius and wisdom of the Hellenic spirit, which was a wholly different human medium from that of the Apostolic age when 'the ignorant stormed the heavens'. The question as to what is 'better' or 'worse' is quite irrelevant. God is actively engaged in these and in all other experiences, and throws his light and shadow upon them. He is likewise engaged in the heresies of Humanism, Liberalism, Communism, and all the other "isms' which mark the revolt of modern man against God, but in which are heard the 'groanings and travailings' of the creature 'waiting for the manifestation of the sons of God'. Man is being deified and humanized through the experience of crises and catastrophies: they represent the apocalypse of God and man, even though they are, or appear to be, a final destruction of Christian values. The fact that this experience is often evidence of the self-assertion of man over against God only serves to restore it in its true religious significance. It urges Christendom to re-examine its position in History and to realize that History is no place for spiritual security and well-being. God denies *Himself* in History through the denials of men; He has submitted Himself to being torn asunder by its riddles and contradictions, and His presence in and power over it is revealed as a transition from Calvary to Resurrection, from death to life. Christians, therefore, should not be too proud in assuming the posture of God's self-appointed defenders *vis-à-vis* the apostate world, for they may thereby find themselves excluded from the mysterious pathways of the providence of God, who is building a new world in and through, and not apart from, the experiences, endeavours, crises, perplexities and denials of a stricken and sinful humanity.

Admittedly, as bare 'fact' or 'datum' the ways of men pertain to the irresistible flux of Time; but as *event* they are charged with transcendent power and actuality and are intensely valid and present here and now, however much they may be removed from us in Time and Space. They are our situation, and we cannot abstract ourselves from it. And the meaning of this, as of every other

situation lies in that God does not abandon us *in it* (not outside of it), while we cannot abandon God *in it* (not somewhere else). We must respond to and accept every challenge with which History confronts us. We must accept the mockeries of Voltaire, the critique of Kant, the dialectic of Hegel, the atheism of Feuerbach, the strictures of Marx, the reclamations of Humanism, Nietzsche's revolt against Christianity, and the nihilistic conclusions of Existentialism; we must equally accept and respond to the revolutionary changes and upheavals which disrupt the seemingly solid ground of human existence, however much we may object to their lawless and godless character. *De te fabula narrata!* All these things are a record of the story of every one of us; and we must go through their purifying fire before attempting to question the world's alleged answers and answer the world's real questions.[1] In all these things man's creative theandric destiny is being fulfilled. His historic deeds and misdeeds and decisions cannot be justified or condemned by way of subjecting them to the tribunal of moral principles, of religion, or of ecclesiastical authority which acts from without. The fact is that this way is primarily responsible for the evils of secularization, of the division of the 'sacred' and the 'profane', which ushered in the rise of man's activity over against God, and for the attempt to affirm autonomously the dignity and value of human creativeness. God is no hierarchical authority which subjects or subordinates the creative life of man. On the contrary, every human act stands and falls in virtue of its intrinsic theandric significance: it cannot be estimated from without, whether by confronting man with ready-made recipes for the problem of his existence or by condemning his endeavours altogether. Berdyaev, who has brought out this issue with great force, observes that even the doctrine of original sin can and has been turned

---

[1] 'Tell me that you are willing to experience your life as a sentence in mankind's autobiography . . . and when you have shown me to what extent you are capable of identification with the rest of mankind, I shall know whether your knowledge is survival knowledge, metanomics of society as a whole, or merely your private metaphysics.' These words, which express the underlying theme of a most remarkable work on the history of European man (Rosenstock-Huessy's *Out of Revolution* to which reference has already been made above) contain a challenge to all those who still believe they can sit as officious observers or as judges of events that are charged with all the force of an historic destiny, affecting everyone irrespective of his or her 'ideology' and modifying everybody's position in History. See also Nicolas Berdyaev's illuminating remarks in *The Fate of Man in the Modern World* on the extent to which we are implicated in the experiences of History.

into a means of degrading man and denying his true vocation, whereas, in point of fact, it is a witness to man's dignity. All these tendencies issue from an implicit or explicit denial of the mystery of God-manhood, and from the ensuing delusion that God's creation is an extinct volcano, a finished product supplied to man in the form of a fixed objective order, 'natural' or 'supernatural'. As a result man is faced with the sole task of conforming respectfully to that order. The idea of evolution was, undoubtedly, a fully justified reaction against such a glorification of static immutability; but it fell itself a victim either to naturalistic determinism or to the 'evil infinity' of an immanental nisus. The human, all-too-human figments of the static, the timeless, the immutable are challenged and called into question not by issueless evolutionism but by Christian theandrism which knows man as a living paradox, the point of intersection of divine and human dimensions, destined to share in and accomplish God's creation and thereby unite past, present and future.

Chapter VII

THE KINGDOM

We must now turn to the idea of the Kingdom of God, already discussed at some length in the first part of this essay. In the preceding chapters we found History to be apocalypse—a progression that gains meaning from an End, from a point of departure, a centre and a goal, which are epitomized in the historical event of supreme divine-human revelation. It is this that gives History the character of a drama which has its acts and its development, its dénouement and its catharsis; it is this also that shows History to be the fulfilment of destiny, the vision of which is a peculiar gift of Israel. God is to come into His own, as in heaven so on earth. This faith found its Christian expression in the witness of the 'Kingdom of God'. The Kingdom is God's, but it is related to History; indeed, it is derived from History as the realm in which God's revelation of Himself occurs.

Nevertheless there seems to be a strange but unmistakable note of pessimism and even bitterness which pervades the New Testament in regard to the affairs of human History. It points —not only in its apocalyptic visions but throughout its entire message—to a shattered world, to a universe that is rent asunder into fragments, or tottering to its ruin, or reserved unto fire against the day of judgment and perdition. Many have attempted —perhaps in self-delusion—to minimize or mitigate these terrible perspectives. But for Christ the world seems to have been as good as finished, and its final state was one of universal failure, not one of proximate perfection that was the nearest thing to paradise: a progress—perhaps, but more like that of the briskly progressive bodies of the Gaderene swine. Blessings on the poor, the afflicted, the oppressed, who perhaps had lost all hope in the world! Woe to the easy, the prosperous, the optimistic, who believed in it because they had themselves found a comfortable place in it. Even the grains of joy in the Gospels and the early

The Kingdom

Church rested on a kind of pessimism. No one can fail to recognize the strange improvidence and irony of the early Christians. No wonder they provoked the indignation of the philistine busybody. They were a long way from those who feel always comfortable and commend religion as an 'indispensable ferment of civilization'.

And yet they also knew: *Work while it is still day!* Life gained a new significance as the arena of 'great tribulation', of the challenge and counter-challenge of Death and Life. The End is coming and is already here, and this spelled: Creation, Incarnation, Calvary, Resurrection, Pentecost, sanctification of all things in God, eschatological fulfilment. God so loved the world that He gave His only begotten Son; He came not to judge but to save the world. They lived and we live in the midst of a fallen, tragically stricken world, in which there is yet revealed a series of divine-human deeds and evidences that have changed man's very existence and his awareness of it, and hence commit him to the task of affirming God's Kingdom in the world as it is. Even Karl Barth says: 'God who judges History is also the God who restores it; and it is confirmed as it passes through God's judgment.' For God's judgment is itself an event of and a crisis in History, however little peace and security it may afford.

Christians are apt to take advantage of eschatological pessimism for their own 'reactionary' ends. The Kingdom of God may be, and indeed is, the wholly 'other', and its otherness and particularity must needs affect our whole vision of life. Evil may be the only force that truly progresses in this world. But do we testify to these truths, or half-truths, or un-truths as they often turn out to be when manipulated by mortal men, because we cannot help being aware of our predicament in History, because we are afflicted when we come to know their tragedy, because, in some sense, we defy them; or because we are devoid of faith and unwilling to receive the challenge of the historic hour and share in God's building of His Kingdom, while at the same time, more often than not, we exhibit a singularly frenzied activity in the feathering of our own little private, social, religious and ecclesiastical nests? 'Those who fight only for success', wrote Tyrrell, 'grow slack when success is hopeless; those who fight for hate or love will fight till they drop. Such indeed has been the energy with which Christian saints have fought: the energy of those who are consumed by their vision of the glory of God, the energy

of those who possessed all things because they lost all things, and those who are masters and not slaves of their purpose.'

The faith of the primitive Church, as the New Testament testifies, was born of an intense expectation of the *parousia* or 'presence' or second coming of Christ 'to judge the quick and the dead'. Jesus Christ Himself has proclaimed what some thought to be His immediate coming and the imminent establishment of His Kingdom. This proclamation is set against the background of tremendous cosmic conflagrations issuing in the destruction of the world.[1] It is significant however that 'the end of the world' is also always 'the second coming' and 'return' of Christ to earth, the revelation of 'the New Jerusalem coming down from heaven' as God's final dwelling place among men, which is to bring the present age or human History to its final climax: '*The kingdoms of this world are become the kingdoms of our Lord, and of his Christ; and he shall reign for ever and ever* (Apoc. xi, 15). History is thus not a void, nor a mere jumping-place from which we can start off into the beyond, but the realm of Christ's kingship.[2]

It is noteworthy that even in the Old Testament, where the messianic kingdom appears to loom in the more or less immediate future, this is linked up with and set in its right perspective by the realization that God's judging and consummating power is revealed in each partial judgment and consummation, so that even when the figure of the sovereign king of David's line is absent the vision of the presence of the Kingdom remains alive. In the New Testament, which purges the messianic idea of all naturalistic associations, the immediacy of the Kingdom is seen in its establishment within man or among men, in the new covenant of God with His people, in Christ's resurrection and the effusion of the Holy Spirit.[3] 'Verily I say unto you, there be some here of them that stand by which shall in no wise taste death till they see the Kingdom of God come with power' (Mark ix, 1).

The image of the Kingdom is further complicated by a whole

---

[1] See the apocalyptic discourse in Mark xiii and the parallel passages in the other Synoptic Gospels. This must be read in conjunction with the wider biblical witness concerning 'realized eschatology' (see above Part I, ch. 4).

[2] Cf. Acts iii, 20-1; 1 Thess. iv, 16; Rom. viii, 20-2; and for the historical implications of Christ's coming: Matt. xiii, 40-1; xxv, 31; John v, 28; etc.

[3] See Charles Gore's discussion of the apocalyptic teaching of the Old and New Testaments in *Belief in Christ*, ch. v.

series of other meanings. It is, as has already been noted earlier on, spoken of as growing, like the growth of a plant and the diffusion of leaven, or as a mixed humanity on earth (Matt. xiii, 33, 47-50, 52), as royal *chrisma*, the anointing of 'eternal life', 'which abideth in you and ye need not that any man teach you' (1 John ii, 27). The character of the Kingdom thus presents a multitude of aspects whose relation is one of tension and co-inherence, and they are resumed in the paradoxical testimony of the Johannine writings to which reference has already been made on several occasions: the final coming is there and yet still the object of expectation.

It is significant that precisely the same biblical experience underlies the liturgical life of the Church, which consists above all of the *anamnesis* of or initiation into the redeeming activity of God. The eucharistic meal is pre-eminently a *kairos*, an 'historic hour'. But the whole Church-year, which epitomizes Christ's 'paschal pathway', His coming from the Father, His life on earth, His death and resurrection, His return to the Father and His abiding presence in and with the Spirit, is a symbol of the *parousia*, an expression of the End of all Time within the course of natural seasons. In the life of the Church past, present and future as it were converge, without at the same time losing their uniqueness, and the Church is placed in the 'nearness' of the living Lord, thereby making Time transparent to Christ's aeon. The tension between existence in Time and fulfilment is, as it were, lifted—at least for a while—and resolves itself in a torrent of joy issuing from the presence of the risen Lord. Yet even this does not annul the eschatological expectation and, indeed, enhances in some sense the longing for universal consummation, since ultimate fulfilment presupposes the presence of the End throughout. 'And the Spirit and the Bride say, come. . . . Even so come, Lord Jesus!' (Apoc. xxii, 17, 20). Christian eschatology will therefore always be an ecclesiology, and, *mutatis mutandis*, Christian ecclesiology is an eschatology. It is the eschatological abiding of Christ through and with the Holy Spirit in the Church, as revealed in its sacramental and liturgical life, rather than its character of a *civitas divina* on earth in the medieval sense, that gives the Church the character of the Kingdom of God and, indeed, of a 'theocracy.'

We must, however, be on guard against reducing the idea of the Kingdom to pietistic or even liturgical *Innerlichkeit*, or moral-

izing, and thus emasculating it, by representing its message as an invitation to men to behave themselves and not to do stupid things, in the manner of Kant, Ritschl, Tolstoy or Harnack and the lesser moralists who persist in preaching at men. Over against this we should remember that there is at least one event in the Gospel story which reveals the *visibility* of the Kingdom of God in the most direct, and not merely allegorical or 'ethical', sense of the word—in anticipation of that ultimate visibility which, as we have seen, is paradoxcially implied in Christ's kenotic presence in the world; it is Our Lord's royal entry into Jerusalem. Here the Kingdom of God that is 'not of this world' is seen as actually, even though as yet partially, realized on earth.[1]

Human existence remains a temporal existence; its temporal character, however, contains the seed of the Kingdom: it is destined to end from within through self-transcendence and thus 'prepare' the coming of the Kingdom. It must end from within as well as from without. The End from without cannot but be destruction; but the End from within is 'construction' or 'reconstruction' and transfiguration. 'Verily, verily I say unto you, that there be some of them that stand here, which shall not taste death, till they have seen the Kingdom of God come with power.'

---

[1] A similar meaning must be attached to the enigmatic witness of the Apocalypse to the thousand-year kingdom (ch. xx, 4-6) which some Christian Fathers (e.g. Justin and Irenaeus) have interpreted in an avowedly chiliastic sense.

Part III

SYMBOLS OF SURVIVAL

Chapter I

DAY AND NIGHT

I t has been one of the principal aims of the present study to show that the three elements which constitute Time—Beginning, Middle and End or Past, Present and Future are more than logical abstractions or the tenses of grammar: they have a transcendent dimension. They can be names for the way in which men experience their place and function in History; they can express men's inmost hopes and aspirations and denote symbols by which responses to life are influenced at the deepest level. Thus it is that each period in History, each nation, even each individual can be viewed as representing and experiencing in various degrees and proportions one or the other of these components of Time. History and historical existence would not be of Time if they did not embody in themselves and represent the rhythm and the antitheses of Time. There are nations whose history is characterized by a peculiar endeavour, both deliberate and instinctive, to relive the Beginning and End of all things, by a readiness to join the two ends of Time, Creation and Apocalypse. And there are those who are, as it were, placed in the midst of Time to build and shape a self-sufficient temporal order. This symbolism of Time as revealed in the threefold character of Beginning, Middle and End may be ignored or taken for granted as always and everywhere the same by the positivistic historian; but we become conscious of its relevance and application the moment we try to gain a deeper understanding of the various elements which make up the movements of History or catch the 'climate' of an historic age, a national development, a society, or a civilization.

There are various ways in which this threefold character of Time can be shown to dominate the stage of human History. It may be said that it owes its special quality to being framed in a number of cosmic symbols whose rhythm is duly revealed in History. Of these the symbols of *Day* and *Night* are the most significant.

167

Symbols of Survival

'And the earth was without form and void; and the darkness was upon the face of the deep. And the Spirit of God moved upon the face of the waters. And God said, Let there be light: and there was light. . . . And God called the light Day, and the darkness he called Night' (Gen. i, 2–5).

Day and Night are no mere fortuitous astronomical phenomena: they provide a mysterious setting for the history of God's dealings with men and of men's dealings with God. They typify and anticipate, as it were, the paths of the creature's destiny.

As we try to gain an insight into human life or examine the movements of History and the rise, growth, and decline of civilizations,[1] we may perceive two underlying forces which operate in them and charge them alike with rhythm and tension: the law of Day and the passion of Night. The law of Day gives human existence form and shape: it limits, orders and defines; it calls for the triumph of reason, logic, lucidity, discursiveness, articulation; it spells achievement and realization. But the light of tame and task-ridden Day is threatened with the coming of nocturnal darkness which breaks the order of diurnal values. Light that seemed omnipotent reveals its innate weakness and superficiality. And man turns to meet the coming Night with her unfathomed mysteries. Night—impenetrable and dark, peopled with horrors, looms suddenly before him, infinitely alluring and full of hitherto unknown promises; and more than the noisy, narrow Day obsessed with the incessant pursuit of perfection, she draws him with her fathomless dimensions. It would seem that the same transcendent power that threw him out into the universe and set him the task of attaining the light of supreme perfection is now turning him in a new direction, where another life awaits him with its unnamed and untried secrets.

We must try to define more closely the relation of these symbols, since it is our conviction that at any given moment of History they represent one or the other aspect of human destiny.[2]

[1] To avoid complex distinctions, I am discarding here the Spenglerian terminology which differentiates between 'culture' and 'civilization', although this may be a fitting way of expressing the thesis set forth in this section. According to Spengler 'civilization' sets in when 'culture' has spent its energies in its own external realizations (*The Decline of the West*).

[2] The 'existential' significance of the symbols of Day and Night has drawn the attention of Karl Jaspers who sees in them a final antinomy of existence and hence eminently transcendent instruments of knowledge (see his *Philosophie*, vol. iii).

Day and Night

However intense the polarity of Day and Night they cannot be viewed out of relation to each other. Their opposition is in some sense invalidated by the very tension that exists between them. As Blake would say, they are not Negations but Contraries. Day is grounded in the depth and lawlessness of Night, and Night resolves herself in the illuminations and fixations of Day. Night may and does admit her own projection and realization in the achievements of diurnal consciousness, while Day receives or seizes the potencies of Night. This relation of Day and Night has received repeated expression in the mythology of mankind, whether in the Genesis myth of revelation, or in the Sumeric legend, reproduced by Plato, of the creation of the world out of Tiamat, or in the Chinese conception of Yin and Yang, describing the rhythmic movement of 'emission' and 'transformation' in the universe.[1]

Every attempt at flouting the law of Day pays the penalty of dissipating man's creatorship and his capacity to build and to achieve. The escape into a 'Kingdom of Ancient Night' may mean a mere refusal to meet the awkward challenge and task of positive activity in the world, a refusal prompted by the elimentary animal instinct which, to use Toynbee's metaphor describing the posture of 'archaism', makes a baby kangaroo in the zoological gardens of a great metropolis take refuge in its mother's pouch after it has been upset by the inquisitive and noisy crowd of human spectators. Day challenges those who tend to eat the bread of idleness, and calls man to responsible acts of creation and achievement; and all human attainments would be rendered meaningless if, through man's unawareness of the law of Day, that very power, Night, which made them possible, is allowed to dissipate them or to reduce them to dust and ashes.

> *Das Unzulaengliche,*
> *Hier wird's Ereignis;*
> *Das Unbeschreibliche,*
> *Hier ist's getan.*[2]

But to forget the Night spells weariness, exhaustion and final inanition. Night may run the risk of chaos and self-destruction; she may involve unbounded passion and naked lust: yet these

---

[1] On this latter conception see Toynbee's *A Study of History*, vol. i. pp. 201–3.

[2] Goethe, *Faust*, ii.

are only some of her transient manifestations. Her real meaning spells no arbitrary destructiveness or nihilism. Night is first and foremost the symbol of depth: she is the realm where man reaches down to the roots of Reality. 'God discovereth deep things out of darkness' and 'his wonders are known in the Night' (Job). Indeed, there are crises which reveal a vehement antagonism of Day and Night, and man is driven to choose the one or the other, to leave Day, whose energies go stale, and dive into the deep of inexhaustible nocturnal being, to beg, as Nietzsche begged, the gods for 'madness', 'to kill the law' or ' to announce to Rome and the world that man is beyond good and evil'; or else he is driven to abandon Night in the exclusive pursuit of surface values, of shallow visible achievement, of 'progress' and 'civilization'.

Night is nearer the Beginning and the End. She is the everlasting reminder of the transcendent dimension of existence, where man is visited by the angels and demons of love and fear, and where his well-protected, well-explored and well-organized middle-of-the-road positions are imperilled. Night is the begetter of Life: 'the Day of the Lord is darkness and not light' (Amos). She is the symbol that draws back the curtain from the Beginning and the End of Time and resuscitates life whenever it has spent itself. Man, shaken and exhausted by the fugitive forms of Time-ridden Day or weary of Day's unending limitations and rationalizations, must dive into the dark of Night, and in so doing he becomes aware of his roots in Reality: he emerges with new power for the fulfilment of his creative vocation in the world.[1]

[1] The symbolism of Night and Day may serve as an analogy for the distinction of 'apophatic' and 'cataphatic' theology. The former is a witness to the fact that God is unknowable and undefinable, and as such penetrates more deeply into the mysteries of divine life than affirmative, discursive statements about it: it is a 'nocturnal' theology which speaks of divine being as *not* being in the sense in which that word is used with regard to the external world, where everything is positively and limitatively determinable. 'And Moses drew near unto the thick darkness where God was (Exod. xx, 21; cf. Deut. iv, 11; Ps. xviii, 11). Cataphatic theology, on the other hand, admits the possibility of attaining a system of knowing God by means of ratiocination: it is a 'diurnal' theology of the finite rather than a theology of the infinitely hidden and groundless mystery of God.

Chapter II

EAST AND WEST

Wherever we look we become conscious of the fact that the conflicts and tensions of human existence can be epitomized in the symbols of Day and Night. We may reduce the diversity of human individuals, of nations and of cultures or cultural periods to two types, one of which stands under the sign of Day, and the other of Night: the one 'critical', the other 'organic' (Saint-Simon); the one governed by the laws of reason, of the finite, of perfect order which at every instant strives to fix in form the irrational flux of life, the other by a longing for life's very irrationality, for its boundlessness and infinitude; the one threatened by the mechanization of life and hence by its dehumanization, the other by the spectre of anarchy which casts destructive shadows across the paths of human existence.

There is perhaps no better historical evidence of the presence of these conflicting and yet correlative elements than the life of Western civilization, compounded as it is of Classical tradition, the Christian spirit, and the influence of the 'external proletariat' (Toynbee) which came from beyond the frontiers of the Roman Empire—Germans, Slavs, Sarmatians, Huns, and other 'barbarians'. All these elements were and in a sense still are interacting and exerting influence on one another.

It has been said not only that the Roman Empire was in essence the embryo of the modern European world, but that Europe to-day is Rome enlarged.[1] It is on the foundations of Graeco-Roman civilization that Europe developed, even though

---

[1] See F. S. Marvin, *The Living Past* and C. F. Strong, *Dynamic Europe*. It would be more exact, in the present context, to speak of 'the West', rather than of 'Europe', or of 'the Western world', which includes its Far-Western outpost on the American Continent. If we apply Toynbee's distinctions this would exclude not only the Eastern world in the strict sense of the term, that is to say, the 'Islamic Society', the 'Hindu Society', and the 'Far-Eastern Society', but also the 'Orthodox-Christian Society' in South-Eastern Europe and Russia (op. cit. vol. i, pp. 34-5).

she may have lost the unity of which this civilization was at once the symbol and the instrument; and it is the Classical genius of Graeco-Roman civilization that informed the way of life of European mankind. Now this civilization is dominated by 'Urizen', the god of law, form and order. Rome established a system of law based on immutable general principles—the 'written reason', exemplifying, perpetuating and applying the philosophical and scientific vision of Greece. Aristotle, the *intellectus agens* of Western Christendom, who expressed and even was responsible for so much in the interplay of ideas and practice in ancient Greece, has been justly called a genius of the golden mean and mediocrity. He was the first to establish the principle that limitation is the index of perfection; and he was as indispensable for the outlook of Western civilization as the organization of the Roman Empire was for the outlook of Western Christendom. But for the 'moderating' influence of Aristotle and the Roman lawyers, Classical civilization would never have obtained the victory over the West.

And yet if Classical civilization had been solely determined by the principles of law and order, it would have exhausted itself and broken down in its earliest stages: actually it owed much to quite different elements, and its peculiar contribution was made possible in virtue of contacts with forces outside the Classicism of Greece and Rome. If Classical culture stands under the sign of Day, of directive reason, form, measure, and limitation, we must yet not forget that it comprises a 'subterranean' stratum and that its compound includes the 'nocturnal' elements of Tragedy, of Eleusian Mysteries, of Orphic myths and Dionysian cults, in fact of *Oriental* forces. Western historians tend to present these as mere 'morbid affections' in the body of the Hellenic society, as symptoms of disintegration: but without them Classical culture would be devoid of its dimension of depth.[1] It is indeed these 'Oriental' elements, rather than Olympian religion or Classical enlightenment and positivism, that gave Hellenic culture its substance, but are so easily discarded or ignored when looked at from the specifically 'Latin' point of view. The Latin mind was quite unable to absorb Hellenism in any profound way: the only thing it did was to spread Greek learning through Western Europe. To the extent, however, to

[1] See E. Jacob, *Der Einfluss des Morgenlandes auf das Abendland* and F. Grenard, *La Primauté de l'Asie*.

which it did absorb it, it was largely a mutilated and stunted Hellenism, as exhibited mainly in Aristotle and the Stoics rather than in Heracleitus, in Plato (the mythologist), and in the Tragedy and Mysteries of ancient Hellas. Rome remained for ever deaf to the song of Orpheus's lyre.[1]

In the present crisis of Western civilization many of its champions completely ignore their own dependence on the forces that have made it a dynamic reality. They are horrified by the irruption of 'Oriental chaos', by the 'tide of Oriental invasion' (James Frazer), which may undermine the apparently stable forms of this civilization and give birth to tragedy. Mythologically speaking this is a new contest between Zeus, who is anxious to keep the world as it is, and Prometheus, who yearns for creative renewal. Western man has come to assume the monopoly of his civilization, regarding the world outside its pale as a sphere of Europe's exclusive cultural, political and economic ascendency, or else dismissing it as without significance for the history of his own civilization.[2] This monopolistic illusion, so brilliantly exposed by Toynbee, issues from one fundamental aberration, namely the political mania of Western man and his inability to penetrate through the superficial plane of politics to the deeper and more vital regions of social and cultural existence. 'By ignoring the cultural plane and by equating politics with life, Western observers arrive at an opinion about non-Western histories which exposes the confusion of their thought as much as it ministers to their self-esteem'.[3] It would seem that only in

[1] The spiritual poverty of indigenous Roman civilization is proverbial. It was natural that this fact should present a constant challenge to foreign religions, whose penetration however did not even bring about a syncretism: they were mostly swallowed up without ever being digested, or else simply suppressed by the Roman State. Nevertheless, 'where the Hellenic Dionysius suffered defeat, the Syriac Christ descended into hell and re-ascended as a victor' (Toynbee, op. cit. vol. ii, p. 285). This victory Gibbon describes, with sorrow and bitterness, as 'the triumph of Barbarism and Religion' over 'the fairest part of the earth and the most civilized portion of mankind'!

Vassili Rozanov said: 'The West is "interested" in life—hence its genius for philosophical ratiocination; the East "endures" life, in pain, in prayer, in praise, in play—hence its genius for religion. But religion will always conquer philosophy.'

[2] See Toynbee's revealing remarks on the implications of the word 'natives' as it has come to be used in Western Europe (op. cit., vol. i, pp. 152-3 and the whole chapter on 'The Misconception of "the Unity of Civilization".')

[2] Toynbee, ibid., p. 165. Toynbee shows however that even on the political

the glorious 'darkness' of the Catholic Middle Ages was the West innocent of this illusion and knew how to resist the vice of cultural *hubris*; though even then, with the close of the first millennium when the apocalyptic expectations of Western Christendom were finally quenched by the spiritual and material victory of Christian Rome, it began already to assert itself in exclusiveness over against the East. May it not be that the unmistakable panic of Western man in face of the 'onslaught of Oriental forces' is due to an incipient inferiority complex and a realization of cultural dissolution at home, although he still remains in the posture of the 'civilized lord of creation', whereby, however, he only dooms himself to be overthrown? At any rate this panic belies his erroneous belief in a static order of things, in an immutable order of Nature, or in the inevitability of progress, a belief so patently untenable in a world that is constantly being reshaped by crises, upheavals and revolutions which overturn the 'diurnal' values of civilization.

In point of fact Night is as perceptible as Day in the alleged stability of European civilization. In almost every period of Europe's cultural development the two contrasting symbols are to be found: they are expressed in the polarization of culture into the 'Apollonian' and the 'Dionysian'—Raphael and Michelangelo, Ingres and Goya, Mozart and Beethoven, Kant and Nietzsche, Pushkin and Dostoevsky, Tennyson and Browning. The one reflecting a world of transparent forms and patterns, a sense of design, of rational articulation, of the supremely civilized; the other full of obscure and inexhaustible forces hurled upon the surface of the world but never acquiring permanent form and, as it were, looming above and beneath all the endeavours of human life.

There was one supreme moment when the fixed confines of Classical civilization were broken and it entered into a life-giving communion with the East: it was the 'Hellenistic' age which saw the Christian Church emerging from the subjugated but until then never really integrated Oriental provinces. Thus it was that Classical civilization 'received its *coup de grâce* from its own mishandled and alienated children' (Toynbee). The 'orientalization' of the West, brought about by the triumph of Christianity, is indeed one of the most characteristic features of

level the picture of the 'unchanging East' in the iron frame of irresponsible despotism is a travesty of the real facts.

the beginning of our era.[1] 'Jerusalem' was victorious over 'Athens' and 'Rome'. 'The glory of God came from the way of the East' (Ezekiel) and the East 'replenished' mankind (Isaiah), for it is the land where God speaks to man—the land of revelation holding within itself the primal sources of life. That is what makes it so terrible and dear. Its visions are kindled by the devouring fire of the Apocalypse—the testimony to the Beginning and End of all things.

The West has seen the attainment of the greatest perfection in the making of civilization; but this very perfection tended to blind its eyes to and made it shrink from the apocalyptic perspectives of History, for in these perspectives yawns at man the abyss of Night—the Night which must inevitably endanger the foundations of every civilization that has grown secure and confident in the finitude of its own achievement.

May it not be that the destiny of the West is to respond to and embody the perennial challenge of the East? May it not be that the West *is* indeed largely that response—a loving or hating response to the regenerating forces of the East, although, or just because, they constantly revolutionize the pathways of Western man and throw his mind completely out of gear? It is surely significant that every time the West attempted to isolate itself within the limits of its 'Classicism' and the boundless 'East' receded from its historical dynamic—be it in the name of triumphant progress towards light and civilization against the onslaught of Oriental darkness or else in mere superior aloofness—the West grew cold and dead. Nobody can blame Western man for his fear of being taken captive. 'An historic day', wrote Berdyaev, 'can never give place to night without huge upheavals and ghastly calamities; it does not give way peacefully.'[2] Historical regeneration always has been and will be marked by large-scale 'barbarization' and a dislocation of the stale and

---

[1] See E. Bevan, *The Hellenistic Age*.

[2] 'The New Middle Ages' in *The End of Our Time*, p. 74; see the whole opening section of this remarkable essay.

I trust that this quotation as well as the whole argument in this chapter are sufficiently clear to avoid confusion with the sensational manner of certain eighteenth-century histories of the Romantic school whose spokesmen wrote of 'sublime Nights' and 'beautiful Days', of 'sublime Seas' and 'beautiful Lands', and other 'sublime' and 'beautiful' things. All this has long ago lost its interest, and we have come to know the terrifying oneness of the historical destiny of men. The everlasting symbols of Night and Day must be seen with this oneness in the background.

worn body social, politic and cultural of man. It is this experience that brings disillusion to the representatives of Western civilization, that makes them complain of the age in which they live, to murmur at the present possessors of power, to lament the past, and to despair or conceive naïve hopes of the future. With sorrow and horror they watch those who, they feel, are like advancing ghostlike legions knocking at the gate of a beleaguered city. But this drifting of the mind to a zone of walking shadows is like erecting a mausoleum over one's own dying body, on which it is written: 'life is a tale told by an idiot, full of sound and fury, signifying nothing' (Macbeth).

Unfortunately, European history has been written largely by those whose main criterion of truth was the illusion of tranquillity or the undesirability of change in a world which is in fact rocked by mighty tempests. The answer to this illusion is that a civilization is doomed to perish unless it succeeds in meeting the challenges of History. It may be said that the problem of History in its apocalyptic and eschatological significance is the dominant issue in the contemporary world and the touch-stone of survival precisely because mankind has reached a stage in which nothing is sufficient to meet the challenge of History but the absolutely creative, complete, final, totally triumphant or totally disastrous, that is, the eschatological solution. Admittedly, it is not easy to show European man, nurtured as he is in the self-confident belief in the perfection or perfectibility of human nature, the validity of such solutions; and he is not likely to be attracted by the spectre of the 'Kingdom of Ancient Night'. And yet History itself seems to have already betrayed his pride and self-confidence and has, in its very crises and ordeals, brought him to the threshold of that Kingdom.

The question is, Can we look at the multiple historical experiences by which mankind is polarized as a piecemeal confusion of isolated developments generating a great amount of temperature but essentially a process 'full of sound and fury, signifying nothing'? Or are these things a living reminder of the End, speaking sometimes with certainty and more often in utter ambiguity, using, like an ironic oracle of doom, its victim as its own mouthpiece? To answer this question in the affirmative is to proclaim History as the Apocalypse: the revelation of a drama to which the only and inescapable clue is the End and in which the 'sound' and 'fury' are shown to be the cipher of

the providence of God as itself an historic process in Time.

There are those, no doubt, who estimate the historical predicament of men in terms of the adjustment of economic, political
or military forces. To such minds the very conception of destiny
in the apparent insignificance and ambiguity of History, and
hence the bringing into relation of human existence with God's
presence and operation in it, is a way of side-tracking the real
facts. There are those who do not underestimate the cogency of
these factors and yet in that very estimation come to know, behind them, in them and before them, an End—another dimension which discloses their real force, their relation to one another
and their true meaning. I do not claim that this knowledge will
correct the aberrations which persistently threaten our world
with disaster. Probably it will not. At any rate I am very far
indeed from drawing religious profit from the misfortunes of
stricken mankind, from attempting to edify others or inviting
them to line up for penitential processions. But if this knowledge
be true, if History is Apocalypse, the realm where God is at
work and man is at work, where the End is coming and is already
here, then we shall not, perhaps, be confounded by the abundance of divine and human tears and curses, of divine and human
smiles and blessings that are needed to live in such a world as
ours.

INDEX

Index

Index